WILLIAM J. KOENIG
WEAPONS OF WORLD WAR 3

WILLIAM J. KOENIG

WEAPONS OF WORLD WAR 3

CRESCENT

A BISON BOOK

*Page 1: West German artillerymen man their
FH-70 155mm gun, a weapon jointly produced by
West Germany, the United Kingdom and Italy.
Page 2–3: an American Minuteman ICBM lifts off.
Page 4–5: the US YAH-64 Advanced Attack
Helicopter is designed with tank-killing as its
main mission.*

© Copyright Bison Books Limited 1981

First English edition published by Bison Books Limited in 1981.

Produced by
Bison Books Limited
4, Cromwell Place
London SW7

Library of Congress Catalog Card Number: 80-27407.

a b c d e f g h

Printed in Hong Kong by Toppan Printing Co., (H.K.) Ltd.

Koenig, William J   1940–
    Weapons of World War III.

    1. Arms and armor.   2. Military art and science.
3. World War III.   I. Title.
U815.K64   355.8'2'09048   80-27407
ISBN 0-517-33004-0

CONTENTS

The twentieth century has already seen two wars which have been of a scale grand enough to merit the term 'world war.' First was the war of 1914–18, which began as a European conflict, but spread to include 22 non-European belligerents, including China, Japan, Siam and last but not least a reluctant United States. In addition to the Western and Eastern Fronts in Europe, battles and campaigns were fought off the coasts of Latin America and in Asia, Africa and the Middle East. Although justified as a 'war to end all wars,' just 20 years later this conflict was followed by a military conflagration on a far greater scale between 1939–45. Some 80,000,000 people bore arms with perhaps 15–20,000,000 killed in combat and untold millions more as civilian casualties. With two such global events recorded in its first half, the twentieth century has taken to numbering its world wars. Thus the 'Great War' of 1914–18 has become World War I, while its successor of 1939–45 has always been known as World War II.

Well before World War II reached its climax over Hiroshima and Nagasaki in August 1945, the specter of World War III already haunted the public consciousness and came to be a central determinant of the postwar international policies and defense postures of the major powers. From the smoke and rubble of World War II emerged two 'superpowers,' which for the last three decades have been armed to the teeth owing to mutual and apparently unallayable fears. Both the United States and the USSR had harnessed their vast resources of manpower and industrial

Overleaf: the Tomahawk Ground Launched Cruise Missile (GLCM) is being developed by the USAF to enhance its theater nuclear capability.

Above right: MiG-21 Fishbed air-superiority fighters operate from a Soviet base. This aircraft is widely used by Frontal Aviation.

Right: the US Navy's F-14 Tomcat fleet-defense fighter is a highly sophisticated warplane which can engage multiple targets simultaneously.

Far right: Soviet SA-4 high-altitude surface-to-air missiles are mobile weapons carried on a tracked launcher vehicle.

capacity to win World War II for the United Nations. While the United States became the 'arsenal of democracy' to equip and sustain much of the Allied war effort, the USSR made a herculean effort to focus its industry on war production and gained the weapons to enable its huge armies to grind down and overwhelm the German invaders. So great were the resources and managerial capacity of the United States that it could fight two major but separate wars in Europe and Asia and still raise its standard of living appreciably. Built with the blood and sweat of its people,

Left: a laser-guided Copperhead artillery shell homes onto its target. Such precision guided munitions are potent antitank weapons.

the Soviet war effort was cruder. Nevertheless it resulted in the emergence of a true superpower with military strength second only to that of the United States, coupled with the confidence born of having beaten the world's most modern and impressive war machine in open battle. The postwar positions of both superpowers thus rested on their military and economic accomplishments in World War II.

The seeds of future world war were sown in World War II and its immediate aftermath. Owing to its distaste for Communism, the United States had been reluctant to take on the USSR as an ally, but accepted the situation because President Roosevelt and Prime Minister Churchill were determined to employ every possible means to defeat Germany. Without the Soviet forces to tie up much of the German ground and air strength, the Allies would have found themselves in a far more difficult situation and could not have defeated Hitler in Europe. Allied policy toward the USSR was to prevent a separate peace between Hitler and Stalin.

There were indeed many problems in the wartime alliance with Stalin. The Soviet leader had made clear his territorial ambitions in Eastern Europe, which were offensive but not necessarily unacceptable to Britain and the United

Right: despite the introduction of a plethora of advanced weapons onto the modern battlefield, the rifle-armed infantryman is still important.

Below: infantry-portable antitank weapons such as this Milan ATGW have helped to redress the balance between armor and infantry.

Far left: the SS-4 Sandal MRBM is one of the early Soviet missiles which is still targeted on Western Europe.

Left: silo-based S-3 IRBMs form part of the French independent nuclear forces.

Right: a Swingfire antitank guided missile is fired from a Striker tracked carrier.

Below: the British radar-guided Rapier SAM has been deployed in defense of RAF airfields in the United Kingdom and Germany.

Above: the Soviet Sagger ATGW can be carried by a two-man infantry team and requires two to four minutes to set up.

States. Stalin for his part was convinced that his allies were delaying the Second Front in Europe so that Germany and the USSR would exhaust each other. The United States and Britain would then be left to dictate the peace, with both Germany and the USSR destroyed. Stalin had as historical precedent the Allied military intervention in the Russian Civil War in 1918–19 aimed at destroying the fledgling Communist regime.

Any illusions harbored by the Allies of postwar cooperation with the USSR were quickly shattered by Soviet expansion in Eastern Europe and Communist pressure in Greece, Turkey and Iran. Churchill in fact coined the term 'Iron Curtain' to describe the postwar Soviet politico-military hegemony over Eastern Europe. The perception of hostile political intent and military threat by each side gave birth to a state of high tension which came to be known as the Cold War. With varying degrees of intensity the Cold War has dominated the foreign and military policies of each side ever since. Tension was particularly strong in the early 1950s when small but very significant wars were fought in Korea and Indochina, while Europeans and Americans worried about the large Soviet armies which were deployed in

Eastern Europe.

The Cold War and its implied resolution in World War III has shaped the postwar period in several important respects. On one hand it has spurred efforts toward the reduction of national sovereignties and the establishment of

world government as represented by the United Nations. On the other hand the lines of conflict between the antagonists have become formalized in competing military alliances and opposing military postures. United States and West European perceptions of the Soviet threat were formalized in the creation of the North Atlantic Treaty Organization (NATO) in 1949. Eventually membership comprised France, West Germany, Britain, the United States, Canada, the Benelux states, Greece, Turkey, Denmark, Italy, Norway, Iceland and Portugal. Military cooperation within NATO was based on similarity of ideology and an international general staff with a permanent headquarters and secretariat was established. The USSR countered with the formation of the Warsaw Pact in 1956, which is made up of itself, Poland, East Germany, Czechoslovakia, Hungary, Romania and Bulgaria. The military impetus behind the two alli-

Below: a French SS-10 wire-guided ATGW is prepared for a test firing during evaluation by the US Army in 1959.

ances was made explicit in 1973 with the beginning of the Mutual Balanced Force Reduction talks, which are aimed at reducing the military presence of each alliance and thus presumably the level of tension and perceived threat in Europe.

The Cold War has led the two super-powers, individually in some areas and together with their allies in others, to shape their military policies with the eventuality of World War III in view. Even so the level and intensity of the preparations have fluctuated. The United States demobilized rapidly after World War II in line with traditional American practice, believing that it could rely on its monopoly of the atomic bomb to deter the Soviet Union and thus reduce spending on conventional forces. Peacetime conscription returned in 1948 however and the conventional forces were rebuilt to fight the Korean War of 1950–53. The forces again atrophied under the 'massive-retaliation' doctrine espoused by President Eisenhower and his Secretary of State John Foster Dulles. By the late 1950s the one-sided emphasis on nuclear weapons as a deterrent looked less effective as the Eisenhower administration began to move toward a more balanced force posture.

The major United States buildup and modernization of the postwar period took place under the tutelage of President Kennedy and Secretary of Defense Robert MacNamara. With the goal of revising United States military policy and strategy, Kennedy stated early in his administration that 'Our defense posture must be both flexible and determined. Any potential aggressor contemplating an attack on any part of the free world with any kind of weapons, conventional or nuclear, must know that our response will be suitable, swift and effective.' Kennedy thus went on to replace the Eisenhower-Dulles strategy of massive retaliation with a strategy of flexible response, or tailoring the application of force to meet specific contingencies. He also propounded the

Below: the Soviet Union has developed a range of mobile surface-to-air missiles to protect advancing armored forces from air attack.

Left: the SH-2 Sea Sprite multipurpose helicopter is carried by US Navy destroyers and smaller ships.

Below: the British aircraft carrier HMS Hermes carries Sea King antisubmarine helicopters and Wessex troop-carrying machines.

Right: a trailer is loaded on a CH-53 Sea Stallion helicopter of the US Marine Corps aboard the amphibious assault ship USS Guadalcanal in 1978.

two and a half wars doctrine, which stated that the United States was to be prepared to fight a major war in both Europe and Asia as well as a smaller conflict elsewhere. The armed forces began to grow rapidly and substantially as the outline of the present United States force posture took shape. The army, for example, reached its current strength of 16 combat-ready divisions, while the present 'strategic triad' of manned bombers, intercontinental ballistic missiles (ICBMs) and missile-carrying submarines took shape.

The armed forces underwent a further spurt of growth and modernization during the Vietnam War, only to be subjected to a period of severe retrenchment in the 1970s by the antimilitary mood of Congress and the public in the wake of the Vietnam debacle. The army has been severely pared down, the number of navy ships reduced by half and major modernization programs such as the MX ICBM, the XM-1 main battle tank, the Trident submarine program and the B-1 bomber either stretched out or, in the case of the B-1, cancelled outright. Programs originally expected to reach fruition in the mid and late 1970s now will not do so until the mid and late 1980s. However, the waning of antimilitary feeling has been coupled with a realization of the magnitude of Soviet military power, which, with events in the Middle East, has resulted in a resurgence of interest in defense and national security as the United States enters the 1980s. This is reflected in the high priority given to defense programs by the Reagan administration in 1981. The coming decade will be a period of major military modernization, but no real force expansion.

Even more than its arch rival, the USSR has been concerned, even obsessed, with its military security and the

Below: nuclear-powered submarines provide almost invulnerable launch platforms for ballistic missiles and also serve as attack submarines.

possibility of a World War III. The declared Soviet position was well put by Marshal Grechko, late Minister of Defense, who wrote 'The aggressive nature of imperialism has not changed and as long as it exists, the threat of a new world war also persists. And there is no other guarantee . . . against its outbreak than strengthening the economic and defensive might of the USSR and . . . raising the combat power of the Soviet Armed Forces and of other fraternal armies.' The Soviet Union has long placed heavy emphasis on highly professional armed forces. From the rag-tag militia formations and elected

officers of the early years of the Bolshevik regime, the Soviets had by 1939 a thoroughly professional military establishment complete with an officer class, rigid rank structure and medals and decorations.

As Marx postulated scientific principles of society, so the early Bolsheviks decided that there were scientific principles of war which can be discovered through study. Thus 'Marxist military doctrine' developed as a combination of emphasis on offensive strategy, belief in the superior spirit of the Soviet soldier and use of political warfare through propaganda, subver-

sion and partisan activity. One feature of Soviet military doctrine that sharply distinguishes it from its Western counterparts is the belief that war and peace are indistinguishable while capitalism still exists and that conflict between socialist and capitalist states is inevitable. Leninist-Stalinist dogma stated that war was a viable instrument

Bottom left: the 16 missile hatches of the nuclear-powered USS Simon Bolivar can be seen behind the sail.

Bottom: the US Navy's nuclear-powered fleet ballistic missile submarine USS Ethan Allen is pictured underway.

Right: a British Army Centurian tank fitted with the Simfire training aid above its 105mm gun. This simulates gunfire with a laser beam.

Below: a Roland SAM fire unit is unloaded from a USAF C-5 transport. This joint Franco-German development has been adopted by the US.

of state policy and that war with the capitalist camp and Communist victory were both inevitable. The advent of nuclear weapons brought a basic change in Soviet doctrine in the mid-1950s. Freed at last from Stalin's rigid military views Nikita Khrushchev abandoned all three of the foregoing tenets. Khrushchev considered that neither war nor Communist victory were inevitable because of the awesome destructive power of nuclear weapons. This Soviet revisionism on military doctrine was one of the main factors in the Sino-Soviet split

Below: an atomic test explosion carried out at Frenchman's Flat, Nevada, by the US Atomic Energy Commission early in 1951.

which began in the late 1950s. Leonid Brezhnev, who succeeded Khrushchev in late 1964, moved toward a somewhat less revisionist position by regarding war as highly undesirable, but realistically possible and in theory winnable.

Soviet force postures have generally responded to these shifts in official dogma. The armed forces shrank from over 12,000,000 men in 1945 to a little over 3,000,000 by around 1960. The large ground and tactical air forces with which the Soviet Union ended World War II remained the center of Stalin's military policy, as he used the threat of Soviet land power against Europe as a counterweight to United States strategic power. Stalin also com-

mitted a major part of scientific and technical resources to military research and development, which was intended to redress the imbalance of power in favor of the Soviet Union. But Stalin refused to allow his military theoreticians to come to grips with the implications of nuclear weapons for all levels of warfare and thus he left to his successors military forces which were equipped and trained only for conventional conflict.

In the belief that any future war would immediately become globally nuclear, the main goal of Khrushchev's military policy was the creation of large medium- and intermediate-range bomber and missile forces in the late 1950s and early 1960s. At the same time a largely unsuccessful effort was made to field a credible ICBM force. Concurrently the large, historically manpower-intensive, Soviet theater forces were drastically reduced in favor of smaller, highly mobile forces, which were considered better able to exploit the conditions of the nuclear battlefield in Europe.

The Brezhnev leadership has pursued a more balanced military policy. It has continued and expanded Khrushchev's stress on strategic programs, but has paralleled these developments with an increase in the war fighting capabilities of the general-purpose forces. The period since the late 1960s has witnessed a truly impressive expansion of Soviet military power, through large increases in force size and weapons capabilities and sophistication. Through sustained effort and massive commitment of resources, the Soviet Union has altered its forces from the peasant horde armed with simple but rugged weapons to a modern, sophisticated war machine. As the editor of *Jane's Armour and Artillery* has observed, 'The days when the Russians had more of everything, but all their equipment was inferior, are over. Their tanks, other armoured vehicles and transport perform as well as – and usually better than – their counterparts in the West.'

Yet despite the fact that World War III has been expected and prepared for in various ways for over 30 years, it has so far been avoided. This has certainly not been from lack of opportunity, as the long list of international crises,

Top: the Vought A-7K is a two-seat conversion of the standard A-7 attack aircraft and it is used to train US Air National Guard pilots.

Above: a US Navy A-6 carrier-borne, all-weather attack aircraft carries a Tomahawk II Medium Range Air-to-Surface Missile.

headed by Berlin and Cuba, can attest. The fear has been that some local conflict would drag in the superpowers and then escalate out of control. Yet neither side is prepared to risk nuclear war for what are really marginal interests in Asia, Africa and Latin America. The incident or situation which ultimately triggers World War III would most likely occur in the Middle East or Europe. Both the United States and USSR have heavy political, economic and military investments in the Middle East and a situation involving Iran and its oil, or even more seriously, a fourth Middle East war, have the potential to involve the superpowers. The strongest United States and Soviet commitments however lie in Europe with NATO and the Warsaw Pact. The military strategy of each is to a large extent focused on defending these commitments. Only the major partners in NATO and the Warsaw Pact have the military strength to create World War III. The war could be triggered anywhere, but ultimately its focus would be Europe, while the United States and USSR duelled at long range with nuclear missiles and bombers.

If World War III were to occur, its focus on Europe would give it continuity with its predecessors. It would also be a total war, as was World War II, in which the harnessing of the national life to war brought complete military defeat. Total war is total victory or total defeat. The end of World War II presaged the future in the use of two small nuclear weapons. The potential belligerents now have stockpiles of tens of thousands of nuclear warheads ranging from artillery shells to giant city busters. While fervently hoping that the war does not 'go nuclear,' both sides assume that it will and prepare accordingly. A nuclear war employing the sophisticated long-range weapons now available would place the survival of civilian populations at extreme risk.

Above: two US Navy F-4 Phantoms escort a Soviet Tu-16 Badger, which overflew the aircraft carrier Kitty Hawk *(background).*

This would continue the trend of the wars of the twentieth century which have become increasingly more destructive of human life and property because of advancing weapons technology and a growing moral nihilism.

War in the twentieth century differs from that of earlier centuries because modern science has greatly improved weapons technologies and military capabilities through the application of chemistry, electronics and physics. Modern electronics has transformed the nature of warfare over some three decades or more, while physics has produced not only 'nukes' but the laser, which will probably have as far reaching an effect on warfare as have nuclear weapons. Science has projected war into space through the development and refinement of various manned and unmanned space vehicles. The application of the advances of science to weaponry has led to a vigorous competition in military hardware, which some believe is almost a surrogate for armed conflict. For as Michael Howard has written, 'It is not in the nature of great powers to acquiesce in the monopoly by their rivals of a major military weapon if they are in a position to acquire it themselves.'

It has been aptly said that attempting to project future forms of war is an uncertain business, but the uncertainty can be reduced by examining the weaponry available to the belligerents. Weapons will largely determine how the war will be fought, because military tactics have often changed with the introduction of new weapons. Thus the products of the current military-technological competition will shape to a large extent the form and outcome of the war. Both sides understand very well that modern warfare demands sophisticated technology and they have accord-

ingly invested heavily in modernizing their arsenals. Possession of modern weapons in quantity is becoming increasingly important because of the time factor in warfare. It is generally thought that a future world war will blow up suddenly and be intensely fought but of relatively short duration, leaving no time to gear up production and fill out inventories. The belligerents will thus have to rely on their existing forces and prior preparations. The preparations will have to be extensive, because the rate of loss will unquestionably be high. In 1973 the Israelis, Egyptians and Syrians lost $3,500,000,000 worth of weapons and related equipment in just 16 days of high-intensity combat.

Certainly the main impact of science on warfare has been the contininuing development of increasingly effective and destructive weapons. Some conventional battlefield weapons now are approaching the destructiveness of small nuclear weapons. These weapons are also much more expensive. Weapons' costs in the United States between 1955–75 grew at approximately five times the rate of inflation. The cost of weapons is becoming as important a factor as their capabilities in determining which weapons are acquired and in what numbers. The rapid pace of technological advance can render expensive new weapons obsolete almost overnight. Cost is thus forcing weapon inventories to become smaller by limiting procurement. This in turn is causing older weapons to be retained in service for longer periods. Much of the weaponry and equipment of NATO and the Warsaw Pact is some 20–30 years old, while the US Navy still has over 30 ships in active service that served in World War II. If World War III should occur in the next decade, the wonder weapons of the 1970s and early 1980s would serve alongside large numbers of weapons from the 1950s and 1960s and even a certain number from World War II.

'There will one day spring from the brain of science a machine or force so fearful in its potentialities, so absolutely terrifying that even man, the fighter, who will dare torture and death in order to inflict torture and death, will be appalled and so abandon war altogether' wrote Thomas Alva Edison. This prolific inventor firmly opposed military application of his work but nevertheless ended up advising the US government on science and technology in World War I. Albert Einstein, whose work provided the theoretical basis of modern atomic physics, replied 'I do not know,' when asked what weapons might be used in World War III, 'but I assure you that World War IV will be fought with stones.' Both Edison and Einstein believed that science in the twentieth century was bringing heretofore inconceivable destructiveness into warfare. The rapid march of technological innovation, particularly since World War II, has created fantastic new military capabilities which are drastically altering the functioning and effectiveness of military forces.

Modern science had its origins in the Renaissance but developed at a slow pace until the twentieth century. Beyond the esoteric art of siegecraft, it contributed little to the technology of warfare until the mid-nineteenth century, nor did the industrial revolution of the nineteenth century owe much to it. There has been more technological development of weapons – steel ships, explosive shells, rifled barrels, the machine gun, the tank, the aircraft and the submarine – to give but a few examples – since 1860 than in all previous history. Since that time, the ability to wage war on a broad scale has also grown through the development of communications, productive capacity, transportation and organizational techniques. However, the real application of science to warfare came when such fields as physics, chemistry and electronics began to be well developed in the early twentieth century.

World War I which so fully ex-

ploited the technology of the industrial revolution to produce the greatest slaughter the world had yet seen, also produced the beginnings of scientific warfare. Many major aspects of scientific warfare appeared and were tested. Two notable examples are the ill-fated experiment with chemical warfare and the extensive use of rudimentary electronic equipment for communications and intelligence purposes. The military exploitation of science and technology, however, did not prosper after the war. In the general postwar revulsion against all things military, scientists focussed on peaceful pursuits while the military establishments of the great powers had only meager budgets. When an employee of the Ordnance Department invented the automatic Garand rifle in the early 1930s, for example, the US Army could not afford to put into production this important advance over the bolt-action Model 1903 Springfield then serving as the standard weapon. As late as 1939, the US Army could spend only 1.2 percent of its budget on weapons research and development. The interwar period thus produced few notable technological advances except for radar.

Scientific warfare blossomed in World War II as all countries, but particularly the United States, recognized the military power latent in scientific knowledge and industrial technique. Scientists of both sides struggled to produce new weapons and methods of warfare and

to counter those developed by the enemy. All countries established government directorates to manage and direct the scientific competition. The United States alone employed some 30,000 scientists and engineers. Heavy reliance was placed on scientific advice to deal with the many problems of the war. Indeed, operations research – the application of scientific techniques to the special problems of weapons and military operations – was born in this period and has flourished ever since. Among the more important scientific achievements of the war were the proximity fuse, penicillin, the explosive RDX (twice as powerful as TNT), the magnetic mine, the first operational jet aircraft and the precursors of the modern cruise missile and ICBM in the German V1 and V2 weapons.

However, apart from the atomic bomb, the weapons of World War II were still rather ineffective. It has been calculated that 300,000 small-arms rounds were necessary to kill a single soldier in World War II. Nor were the weapons particularly destructive. Even the 12,000-pound 'blockbuster' bombs had a limited radius of effects relative to the amount of explosive power used.

Since World War II, however, weapons development has been extremely rapid. Nuclear weapons, whose exist-

Below: an overall view of the computer complex at Ellsworth AFB, demonstrates the widespread military use of automatic data processing.

Overleaf: these rows of computer systems are installed inside the North American Air Defense Command Post in Cheyenne Mountain.

ence has forced many traditional assumptions about warfare to change, now range from huge city busters to small battlefield weapons ('mininukes') and provide the ultimate firepower in warfare. While nuclear weapons have tended to dominate military thought since World War II, dramatic advances in conventional weapons have also occurred. These advances have been made possible in part by the rapid advances in component miniaturization, computers, small-engine design, efficient new fuels, guidance and sensor technologies, electronics and many other areas over the past three decades.

The rapid and extensive exploitation of these technological advances has occurred partly because the process of military innovation for each side has been institutionalized since World War II, one of the most important legacies of that conflict to the postwar period. This institutionalization of large-scale military research and development stems directly from the postwar Soviet-American politico-military competition. In his widely read book *Military Strategy*, the Soviet Marshal V D Sokolovsky, for example, wrote that 'the problem of assuring quantitative and qualitative military-technological superiority over the probable aggressor' requires *inter alia* 'the broadest enlistment of the forces of science and technology.' Some observers have in fact suggested that the competitive process of military innovation represents a

surrogate for large-scale warfare between the two superpowers.

Both superpowers have invested heavily in new technologies for military applications because the price of being clearly inferior in a nuclear world could be catastrophic. In 1979 the US Department of Defense spent over 10 percent of its budget on military research and development. In the United States at least, the procurement of advanced new weapons has also become highly politicized. Major battles take place in Congress over which weapons to select while the issue of a new ICBM and strategic bomber became major points during the 1980 presidential campaign.

The impact of science on contemporary warfare is most visible in firepower, communications and mobility. Large and very accurate amounts of fire can be delivered routinely on targets because of the advance of guidance, control and sensor technologies. Communications have now developed to the point where tactical operations in remote places can be directed by highly centralized authorities halfway around the world. Mobility, as will be seen, has greatly expanded the spatial and temporal dimensions of warfare, even to inner space. These changes have been made possible,

Below: weather advisors operate their computer consoles at the USAF Global Weather Central at Offutt AFB, Nebraska.

directly or indirectly, by the development of the computer, yet another legacy of World War II.

The industrial revolution marked a major watershed in socio-economic development by magnifying the power of human muscles through the mechanization of labor. The computer has already begun to revolutionize the social organization of modern societies by magnifying the power of the human brain. Machines now do in tiny fractions of a second tasks which would take humans a decade or more. They make possible the storage, retrieval, and manipulation of immense bodies of data. A relatively straightforward, small study of newborn infants conducted by a psychologist and her four assistants in a two-month period in 1974, for example, produced over 300,000 pieces of discrete data which would have been nearly impossible to organize and analyze without the aid of a computer. Indeed, computers were developed in response to the large amounts of information which needed to be processed in World War II.

One of the most striking aspects of the twentieth century is the incredible growth of information in almost all areas. The explosion of information is exemplified by the fact that one in 160 American workers in 1870 performed clerical functions whereas one in four does so in 1981. The problem of coping with an excess of information stretches back at least to the ancient Egyptians and Babylonians who used the abacus as their instrument of mechanical data processing. The origins of the computer really date from 1847 when an Englishman named John Boole devised a system for expressing logic (formal reasoning) in simple mathematical terms. This logic, together with his related algebra, is still used in designing computer circuitry. A second important input to the development of the computer appeared in the 1880s in the Hollerith Code. This simple mechanized process could sort 50–80 punch-coded cards per minute. Its first serious application was in the tabulation of the 1890 census where it reduced the time involved from the eight years required for the 1880 census to two and a half years. The final essential element of the

computer came in 1904 with the invention of the diode tube by John Fleming, another Englishman, which enabled alternating current to be changed to direct current.

Forty years later, the first automatic computer was developed at Harvard under army sponsorship. Called the Harvard Mark I, this creature could perform addition and subtraction in .3 seconds, store 23-digit/decimal numbers, and perform long sequences of logical and arithmetic operations. It was followed in 1946 by ENIAC (Electronic Numerical Integrator and Calculator), again under army sponsorship. Filling several very large rooms and requiring 140,000 watts of electricity for its 18,000 vacuum tubes, ENIAC could perform 5000 calculations per second involving 10-digit/decimal numbers.

Since the debut of ENIAC, computers have rapidly increased in capacity and equally rapidly decreased in size and power requirements. The first major change to ENIAC-type machines stemmed from the development of the transistor in 1957 and with it the beginnings of solid-state circuitry. In contrast to the huge descendants of ENIAC, what is now called the second generation of computers were notably smaller, used far less power, and had magnetic storage and easily interchangable printed circuit boards. Performing their tasks in millionths of a second, they were operationally much more reliable.

Technological advance in the form of microcircuitry has brought on a third generation of computers since 1964. First, complete circuits were printed on silicon chips half the size of a fingernail, then thousands of circuits were printed on one one-quarter-inch square chip (large-scale integrated circuitry) and, since the late 1970s microprocessors or entire 'computers on a chip' have appeared. Coming by the mid-1980s is very large-scale integrated circuitry with up to 100,000 circuits on one chip and the end is nowhere in sight. Component miniaturization now allows computers with the power of ENIAC to fit in a coat pocket and is making computers cheaper to produce and operate. These machines are thus being introduced into all aspects of modern life – the home, schools, government, business and communications – at an increasing rate.

The military has also wholeheartedly embraced the computer. The US Department of Defense owns more than half of the computers in the US government while there is hardly any modern military system that does not involve some aspect of a computer. Computer technology has been linked with sensor devices such as radar, infrared, electro-optical, TV, photo-graphic and electronic intercept to produce modern command and control, warning, fire control, and battle-management systems which, in their aggregate, have been largely responsible for transforming the face of modern warfare.

These systems have accelerated the time and extended the geographic dimensions of combat and strategy. In the past, response to the course of operations or strategic moves by the enemy did not have to be immediate. Decisions could be taken or implemented hours or even days later. Now the speed and accuracy of modern weapons demand response in minutes and seconds. The 6000-mile track of an ICBM takes 30 minutes, a submarine-launched ballistic missile may arrive on target in less than 10 minutes while the US Army's Pershing II missile, to be based in Central Europe, will strike Soviet targets in somewhat less than 10 minutes from launch. For systems designed to defend against these weapons, time exists in perhaps millionths of a second as trajectory data from radars and infrared sensors is analysed, intercept courses computed and interceptor missiles launched by computers.

Computers thus manage the information produced by sensors to compute intercepts and course corrections and to control the performance of weapons systems. The small digital computer in the fire-control system of the Abrams tank, for example, takes data from the laser range finder

Below: a cutaway drawing of the E-3A showing its internal equipment layout. The aircraft carries a 17-man crew.

Below right: the US E-3A Airborne Warning and Control System carries a powerful radar scanner above its fuselage.

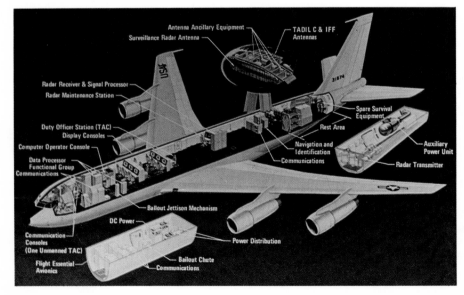

and lays and fires the gun in a fraction of a second. In the now-deactivated Nike-X antiballistic missile system, a high-performance radar located the incoming ICBM warhead, a high-speed computer solved the intercept problem and launched a high-acceleration Sprint missile within minutes. After travelling over 240,000 miles, American lunar probes land within five miles of their targeted landing areas. The precision guidance of ICBMs and space vehicles and satellites is possible only because of high-speed computers.

One of the most important marriages of the computer has been with communications systems. The same technical advances which have caused the rapid evolution of the computer are also transforming communications technology. Transmission systems for some time have been in the process of 'digitization,' that is, functions which used to be performed in analog circuits are now performed digitally in mini-computers or microcomputers. There is, in the words of one authority, 'an inevitable trend of communications systems toward being a collection of computers netted together.'

The rapidly growing use of automation to control communications circuits has had a profound impact on the military function known as command and control or C^2. Command is the process of making a decision and control is the execution of that decision. Since the dawn of organized warfare, command and control have been a key

Above: an interior view of a C-130 airborne command post showing air controllers at their stations during a joint USAF/US Navy exercise.

to military success. As the scope of war expanded beyond the immediate battle-field, so also did the need for military intelligence and communications. As communications technology has developed, the tactical commander has increasingly lost the authority to take the initiative. Abraham Lincoln, less than 100 miles from Gettysburg, could only send General George Meade a wire on the morning of 1 July 1863 asking to be informed of the outcome of the engagement with Robert E Lee's invading southern forces. Meade was in

complete tactical command. By contrast, consider President Lyndon Johnson in the White House situation room personally directing the operations of the US Sixth Fleet in the eastern Mediterranean with one hand on the hot line to Moscow in 1967. Or consider Secretary of State Henry Kissinger issuing tactical orders to battalion commanders during the 1975 *Mayaguez* rescue operation, or President Jimmy Carter talking directly to the field commanders of the ill-fated Iran rescue mission in 1980 and personally issuing the order to halt the operation.

Instantaneous communications and information have led to the ultimate centralization of the command function. The highest authorities now become involved in remote tactical operations. This centralization means that all political and military events are interconnected because each side assumes that the other is fully aware of all the implications of its actions. The trend for both sides has been to develop immense computerized command and control systems, with the key being high-speed communications and data-processing capabilities. Communications are such an integral part of command and control that the whole package is usually referred to as 'command, control and communications' or C^3. C^3 really came of age in the 1970s after many minor and a few major communications disasters in the preceding

Above: the Tu-126 is the Soviet equivalent of the US E-3A, but it is of questionable effectiveness in this role.

decade. The two best known of these involved the USS *Liberty*, an intelligence-gathering ship, which was fired on by Israeli gunboats in 1967 because it failed to get information warning it away from a sensitive area, and the USS *Pueblo*, a similar ship, which was captured when a computer misrouted a message warning of impending North Korean attack.

The United States has built a standardized C³ system to be used by all military commands – the World Wide Military Command and Control System (WWMCCS, pronounced Wimex). This is a global network of satellites, radar stations, other sensors and warning and communications systems controlled by a huge network of computers. The President and Joint Chiefs of Staff use the Wimex system to warn of attacks and coordinate and control all activity by the US forces anywhere in the world.

Apart from Wimex, the US Air Force has the largest C³ apparatus of the forces. The centerpiece of the Air Force system is the Single Integrated Operations Plan (SIOP), a computerized masterplan for all Air Force operations in the event of World War III.

Computers have been an integral aspect of the military scene at the strategic level for over two decades, but now promise to assume the same role at the tactical level. Owing to the reduction in size and power requirements in computers, battlefield computers are now feasible and are being developed at a rapid rate. By the mid-1980s there will be a proliferation of automatic data-processing devices on the battlefield which ensure the fast flow of information to all levels of command. Thus the tactical command post on the battlefield of the future will employ a computer to keep track of the tactical situation, have automated analysis and display of intelligence information and computerized logistics and message centers. If one computer in

this system is degraded or knocked out, the others will pick up its function in a process called interoperability. At the theater level, the rapid synthesis of reconnaissance information by computers is being developed to provide commanders with the capability to make decisions on the basis of real-time (that is, as it is happening) intelligence. The survivability of the command and control function is being increased by making command posts mobile and the use of AWACS (airborne warning and control system) aircraft as alternate airborne command posts.

Military forces have become so dependent on their electronic systems that their combat capability can be substantially reduced or even altogether eliminated by attacking and degrading these systems. In a recent report, the US Defense Science Board commented on the advent of the 'electronic battlefield where the classical function of command, control and communications has become almost completely dependent on electronic devices. A wide

tronic aspects of the 1973 war has brought a number of changes in electronic warfare. For example, radar-directed weapons now incorporate 'frequency agility,' that is, the ability to vary their radar frequencies to make point jamming more difficult. In response, computer-directed jamming systems have been developed to improve reaction time against frequency agility.

Over the years, both sides have invested considerable energy and ingenuity in gathering as much knowledge as possible about each other's electronics and radars. 'Elint' or electronic intelligence is gathered by various platforms – ships, aircraft, and satellites – as each side tries to catalogue the radar signals of the other and establish the opposing electronic order of battle. Elint-configured versions of the Soviet Tu-95 Bear long-range bomber regularly fly off the east coast of the United States and off northern Europe, probing air defenses and gathering electronic intelligence. The United States and its allies use a variety of platforms, including the mach 3 SR-71 Blackbird, for the same functions. Over 100 US airmen have been lost in the constant probing of Sovet air defenses.

Since a Soviet SA-2 surface-to-air missile brought down Francis Gary Powers and his U-2 reconnaissance aircraft in 1960, photographic intelligence has been gathered by satellite over hostile territory. At least four U-2s are known to have been shot down over China. The U-2 is still in service, however, and is still used effectively for a variety of reconnaissance missions.

Hardware used in the electronic battle includes ARM (antiradiation missiles) which home in on enemy electromagnetic emitters such as air-defense radars. These were used effectively against North Vietnamese radars during American air operations over North Vietnam. The only North Vietnamese defense was to turn off their anti-aircraft radars for much of the attack. The most advanced development in this area is the US Air Force's F-4G Wild Weasel system, which detects, identifies, locates and attacks enemy electromagnetic emitters and now

variety of sophisticated sensors are needed to observe the state of the battle, computers are required to rapidly process information to assist in the decision process, and rapid communications must be used to convey almost instantly the command to control forces. With this extreme dependence on electronics, it is not surprising to find the emergence of weapons to disrupt or exploit its use.'

Counter C^3 operations, as they are known, have thus become a primary mission for each side. By attacking communications, surveillance, targeting and weapon-guidance systems, the number of weapons ultimately arriving on target is reduced, while defensive capabilities can also be degraded through jamming, deception and physical attack of sensor and C^3 systems. Thus the attack and defense plans of each side must include high-priority C^3 targets. This in turn requires advance detailed knowledge of the enemy 'electronic order of battle' and careful preplanning because the pace of the battle may be very swift. The crucial role of C^3 is best illustrated by the words of a US general who suggested that the 'winner of the next war would be the side with the last two antennas standing!'

Beyond degrading or destroying C^3 systems, however, electronic warfare or the 'battle of the beams' extends over a wide spectrum of activity. The Soviets made effective use of chaff and jamming to mask the movements of their forces from NATO radars and communications monitors during the 1968 invasion of Czechoslovakia. It was, however, the crucial role of electronic warfare in the 1973 Arab-Israeli War that really shaped the attitudes and doctrine of the United States, European and Soviet forces. In this conflict, there was extensive monitoring of enemy communications by each side, widespread 'point' jamming of radars whose frequencies were known or could be determined and successful use of 'barrage' jamming to disturb the tactical communications of the opposing armored formations. Study of the elec-

Left: a Pave Sword laser designator pod mounted on a USAF F-4 fighter at Ubon, Thailand, during the Vietnam War.

Below left: an F-102 interceptor escorts a Soviet Tu-95 Bear off the coast of Iceland, as the latter attempts to monitor NATO fleet exercises in the area.

Below: an F-4C from the USAF Flight Test Center fires a Bullpup AGM, an example of an early precision-guided munition.

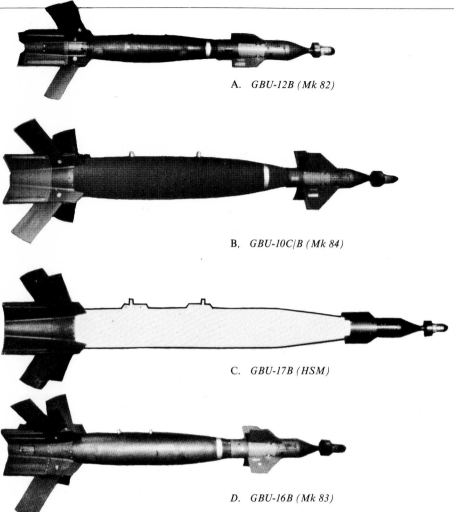

A. *GBU-12B (Mk 82)*

B. *GBU-10C/B (Mk 84)*

C. *GBU-17B (HSM)*

D. *GBU-16B (Mk 83)*

carries a high-speed ARM. Modern warplanes are now equipped with ECM (electronic countermeasures) pods which carry jamming equipment, chaff, and flares to match the infrared spectrum of the aircraft to counter the radar and infrared seekers of enemy missiles. The newest ECM pods are programmed, so that the threat-warning system of the aircraft can direct the pod to meet the most immediate threat. Every development brings a counter-development, however, and both sides are now hard at work on ECCM (electronic counter countermeasures). The electronic battle goes on in peacetime with each new system development giving one side at least some theoretical advantage.

While electronics has revolutionized the command and control function, it is also profoundly affecting fire control and the nature of firepower. Since the advent of firearms in warfare, most of shots fired have missed. It was only in

the mid-nineteenth century that rifled weapons began to transform warfare with their accuracy and greater ranges. Before this happened, as Ulysses S Grant said of the smoothbore musket, 'At the distance of a few hundred yards, a man might fire at you all day without your finding out.' After accuracy came ever-higher rates of fire through mechanization, breechloading and single case shells. But unless the target could be seen or, in the case of artillery, its location known, there were limits to the increase in lethality which accuracy and rate of fire could bring. Thus gunners were forced to saturate targets with a very high volume of fire with a low kill probability per shell. In World War II, for example, 3.5–4 tons of bombs and shells were expended per enemy casualty in the Italian campaign, while in the Vietnam war, an estimated 27,000 rounds of ammunition were fired for every Viet Cong killed.

Electronics, however, has now made

possible much higher levels of lethality for conventional weapons by a combination of sensing in the electromagnetic spectrum and control through solid-state electronic devices. A whole new category of weapons, called precision-guided munitions (PGMs), has appeared, been tested in two wars already, and promises to significantly alter the nature of a future world war. PGMs result from new methods of target detection and location on the battlefield – radar, sonar, radio direction finding, infrared and TV, among others – that can be exploited with small, relatively simply computers to integrate target data for fire control. Indeed, the current trend in fire control is for less and less human participation. Any electromechanical weapon which corrects its course in flight to achieve a better than 50 percent hit probability at full range is considered a PGM. Precision is, of course, relative for any given PGM and will depend on such factors as target characteristics, warhead capabilities and the extent of target damage required. There is a wide range of performance as many PGMs are in fact far from precise.

As with so many other seemingly new developments in weaponry, PGMs are not in fact so recent. In World War I there was experimentation with flying bombs with preset controls (the 'Kettering Bug') but none were ever employed in combat. In World War II the United States developed a number of air-to-ground tactical PGMs. The Army Air Force had the GB-1, a 2000-pound bomb with attached aerodynamic surfaces and preset controls. A raid in May 1944 saw 116 of these weapons launched against Cologne. The radio-guided azimuth only (AZON) bomb was used extensively in Burma for the specialized task of bridge busting. As early as 1938 the US Navy was experimenting with radio controlled drones and TV guidance from control planes. There was some limited testing of these drone bombs in peripheral combat zones of the Pacific, but the program was never allowed a serious operational test. Another Navy PGM, the radar-guided Bat missile, actually sank a Japanese destroyer in April 1945. The United States and its allies also experimented with heat-seeking, light-seeking and TV-guided bombs during the war.

The Germans also produced operational PGMs. The V1 and V2 missiles were directed weapons, but not true PGMs. Dr Herbert Wagner and his colleagues at the Henschel Aircraft Company developed the Hs-293, an air-to-surface missile with solid-fuel rocket engines, radio control and visual guidance. This weapon successfully attacked British ships in the Bay of Biscay in 1943. Employed in the Mediterranean, the SD1400X or 'Fritz X' missile was radio controlled through a trailing wire and sank first HMS *Egret* and then the Italian battleship *Roma* as it attempted to defect to the Allies. Despite these successes, however, the control planes for these guided weapons were sitting ducks for Allied fighters and the German PGM threat was eliminated within six months.

In the postwar period nuclear weapons dominated military thought and, despite their demonstrable wartime accomplishments, the further development of PGMs essentially came to an end. It was only in the late 1950s and early 1960s that the armed forces of the great powers tended to re-emphasize conventional weapons as they belatedly realized that a wide range of military contingencies existed for which nuclear weapons were neither appropriate nor even effective. During the Lebanon crisis of 1958, for example, the US Air Force learned of the problems of forces structured entirely around nuclear weapons. 'There is considerable doubt as to the conventional combat capability of the F-100 units,' stated one Air Force report. 'Only a few of the F-100 pilots had strafed; none had shot rockets or delivered conventional bombs.'

Largely in response to the demonstrable effectiveness of the Soviet SA-2 surface-to-air missile (SAM) in bringing down Powers' U-2, the Air Force began to deploy its first PGM of recent times, the Shrike antiradar missile, in 1964. The first conflict in which PGMs were

Above: a close-up view of a laser tracker mounted on an A-10 close-support aircraft at Edwards Air Force Base, California.

used to a significant extent was the Vietnam conflict of 1965–72. Laser-guided bombs of the Paveway family were used to attack North Vietnamese truck traffic in Laos in the late 1960s. Soon thereafter, electro-optically guided bombs known as HOBOs, (homing optical bombs) were in use as well. The high point of PGM use came on 16 May 1972 when a single sortie by F-4 Phantoms destroyed the vital Thanh Hoa bridge, after between 450 and 600 previous sorties had failed at a cost of at least 18 planes and several hundred thousand pounds of conventional bombs. PGM advocates have seized on this example in particular to illustrate the relative operational and cost effectiveness of guided over unguided weapons against heavily defended point targets.

The Vietnam War, however, sheds light on other, less complimentary aspects of PGMs. One of the earliest postwar PGMs, the Soviet SA-2 SAM, was widely deployed by the North Vietnamese in point defense of their high-value targets. US Air Force data shows that in the early years of air operations over North Vietnam an average of 50 SA-2s was required to down one US plane and after 1968 the figure rose to 100 per plane. First deployed in the late 1950s, the SA-2 is, technologically speaking, a first generation SAM and was designed to intercept bombers incapable of high

maneuverability. It proved to have low operational effectiveness against highly maneuverable tactical aircraft. American pilots for the most part simply outflew the SA-2 missiles, but they also attacked the system's radars with ARMs to force them to shut down and used point jamming as well. Although the North Vietnamese adopted countermeasures such as mobility, camouflage, and optical tracking, they were unable to raise the level of effectiveness because of the inherent limitations of the SA-2. Even against B-52s, the system proved unable to cope with simple evasive maneuvers. What the SA-2 defenses did accomplish was to force a significant portion of United States air assets to be devoted to defense suppression and this in itself was an important contribution. The important lesson to be learned from the air war over North Vietnam is that the side with the more up-to-date weapons will enjoy significant advantages over its opponents in any given area of combat.

Coming on the heels of the apparent PGM successes in Vietnam, the role of PGMs in the 1973 Middle East War firmly established their place in the arsenals of the 1980s and caused some observers to see them as the determining factor in future warfare. In 1973 the

Above: the AIM-9 Sidewinder air-to-air missile homes onto the heat emitted by the target aircraft's engines.

Egyptians made extensive use of PGMs, while the Israelis were notable for their success in devising effective countermeasures. Indeed, the 1973 conflict was far more indicative of the true potential of PGMs because both sides were well armed with modern weapons. The Egyptians were well-equipped with the Soviet wire-guided Sagger antitank guided missile, the man-portable SA-7 Strela SAM that for the first time offered the infantry a credible immediate defense against low-flying aircraft, and the SA-6 tactical SAM which represented a considerable technological improvement over the SA-2.

In the early phase of the war, these weapons seemed to be having a decisive effect on the tide of battle, as Israeli air and armor tactics took no account of their presence. But the initial effectiveness of the PGMs caused the Israelis to devise new tactics and in the end PGMs had only a marginal effect on the war's outcome. The Sagger caused less than a quarter of Israeli tank losses, and these mainly early in the war. Of the 3000 Arab and Israeli tanks destroyed during the war, at least 80 percent succumbed to other tanks, despite the thousands of antitank guided missiles expended. The tank was the ultimate engine of Israeli victory because the Israelis used smoke,

maneuver and suppressive fire to neutralize the enemy PGMs.

The SAMs, intended to guarantee local air superiority, fared little better. An estimated 5000 SA-7 firings served to down only four planes, while the SA-6 proved to have similar limitations to those of the SA-2. Although much more resistant to ECM, the SA-6 was still outmaneuvered by aircraft and still vulnerable to suppressive attack and ARMs. Indeed, the largest single cause of Israeli aircraft losses was traditional antiaircraft fire in the form of the ZSU-23-4, a tracked, radar-directed, quad-barrelled gun system.

Yet the vision of the diminutive Sagger smashing Israeli tanks in 1973 has made a lasting impression on many analysts and raised quite unrealistic expectations of low-cost, precision warfare in the future. In combination with new battlefield sensors, C^3 systems and more lethal warheads, PGM advocates argue that 'what can be seen, can be hit, and what can be hit, can be destroyed.' The greatest hopes for PGMs are focussed on Central Europe, where numerically inferior NATO forces plan to use various 'force multipliers' to neutralize the advantage of more numerous Warsaw Pact forces. The official position is that NATO need not match the Warsaw Pact tank for tank and missile for missile because PGMs have great potential for force multiplication. With appropriate intelligence and delivery support, PGMs 'can make

the battlefield untenable for most modern forces' states one report.

What PGMs in fact offer in warfare is to substitute far fewer but much more expensive and sophisticated projectiles, manned by far fewer (sometimes only one) soldiers, for the large volume of fire from many unguided weapons which has heretofore been necessary to neutralize a target. PGMs have clearly demonstrated their effectiveness on the battlefield, but at the same time revealed severe limitations. They have, for example, a lower rate of fire and slower time to target than gunfire and thus leave their crews vulnerable. Target acquisition is the key to their effectiveness, but almost all current PGMs require a clear view of their target. Their effectiveness can be reduced by smoke, dust, bad weather, concealment, darkness, terrain and other factors. PGM firepower remains very important because in actual battle conditions, hit probability may not be the 80–90 percent of the test ranges but as low as 10 percent.

What is in fact occurring between NATO and the Warsaw Pact reflects the dynamics of the 1973 war. After the initial impact of PGMs on the military scene, countermeasures of various sorts have been devised to exploit their inherent weaknesses. PGMs themselves are now being improved to counter the countermeasures which will in turn undoubtedly adapt further and the cycle will continue. While PGMs will not revolutionize warfare as their more extreme enthusiasts claim, there can be little doubt that they are an important and permanent fixture in modern weaponry and as such will bring significant changes to the battlefields of the future.

PGMs really emerged as a distinctive family of weapons in the late 1960s and early 1970s. The late 1980s and early 1990s are probably going to see the emergence of another distinctive family of weapons, a family which may affect war far more profoundly than have PGMs – the family of weapons known generally as 'directed-energy' weapons, which refers to lasers and particle beams. Laser stands for Light Amplification by Stimulated Emission of Radiation, while particle-beam tech-

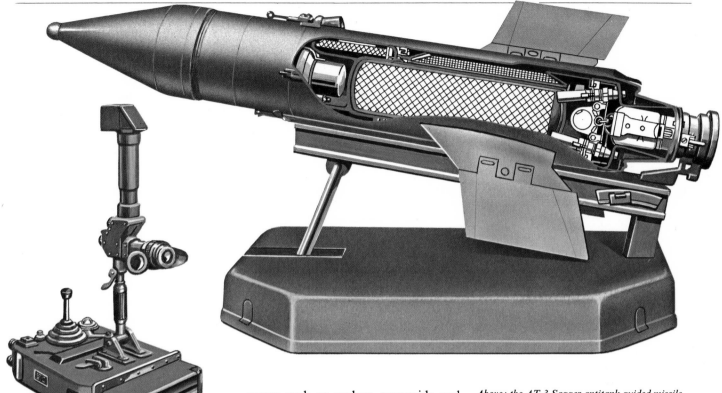

nology is closely related to the work on nuclear fusion for commercial applications. Particle-beam technology is in the early stages of research and exploration, but lasers have been in widespread use for many years in areas such as navigation, supermarket checkout-code readers, surveying instruments, medicine and, most recently, fiber-optic communication systems. These are low-energy lasers employing only a few watts of laser power. Industrial lasers of up to 20,000 watts can cut a one-inch steel plate at the rate of several inches per minute.

Einstein outlined the theoretical basis of lasers in 1916, but the first lasers were developed in the late 1950s and early 1960s. Whereas ordinary light is noncoherent, the laser emits coherent light, that is light waves that are perfectly aligned. Many materials have been used to produce 'lasing' action. The high-energy lasers used in industry and now being developed as weapons are mostly 'gas dynamic' lasers. Two

Right: a close-up view of an electric discharge convection laser undergoing testing under laboratory conditions.

gasses such as carbon monoxide and oxygen are burned at very high temperatures to create a new gas, carbon dioxide in this case. As the gas cools, its molecules radiate laser light which is collected by two facing mirrors. These reflect the light into a lens which focusses them into a narrow intense beam. Lasers are the only product of high-energy physics to have practical military applications since the development of nuclear weapons in the early 1940s and may ultimately come to have a similar impact on warfare.

Above: the AT-3 Sagger antitank guided missile has been mounted on helicopters, reconnaissance vehicles and armored personnel carriers.

Lasers are seen as primarily defensive systems able to fulfill air-defense missions that to date have been nearly impossible. It is hoped that lasers will provide the long-sought defense against ballistic missiles. Because laser light travels at the speed of light (186,000 miles per second), the time to target of laser weapons is virtually instantaneous. Laser light thus travels a mile in six

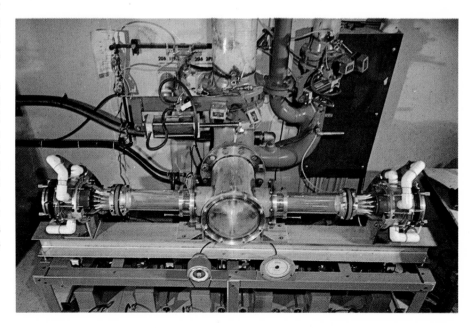

millionths of a second, during which time an aircraft travelling at mach 2 will move about one eighth of an inch and an ICBM about one inch. Once locked on target, therefore, the laser weapon is virtually certain to hit the target. Lasers also produce no recoil and can make rapid directional changes from one target to another. But to 'kill' their targets, laser systems with two to five million watts of energy must focus their light on the target (the 'dwell time' of the system) until it vaporizes, has a hole melted in it, or its electronic package is affected. It is in fact thought that the first operational laser weapons will be those which are designed to destroy the seeker, sensors, or radome of the target rather than the whole platform itself.

Disadvantages of lasers are thus that they require large amounts of power, pinpoint aiming, and a certain dwell time. The fire-control system would have to be able to keep the beam focussed on the same point on the target, then know when the target had been disabled or destroyed, and move on to another target. Lasers will be more effective weapons in space than in the earth's atmosphere, where water vapor, clouds, dust and other particulate matter cause the beam to 'bloom' or have lower intensity and lose focus, thus increasing the dwell time. Because of the blooming problem, lasers may not be practical weapons much below 35,000 feet where 99 per cent of the water vapor in the atmosphere is concentrated.

There are in fact a number of articulate critics who question the feasibility of lasers as weapons on the grounds of practicality and the fact that countermeasures to thwart lasers appear to be as simple as placing dust, smoke or water vapor in the path of the beam. One anonymous but widely quoted critic said, 'A laser big enough to do militarily significant damage would be so big it wouldn't have to work – just drop it on the enemy.'

However the feasibility of laser weapons has already been demonstrated. The US Air Force, Army and Navy all shot down drones and tactical missiles on test ranges with lasers during the 1970s. In 1980 the Air Force tested a gas dynamic laser mounted on a modified KC-135 jet tanker against air-to-air missiles. With a 23-inch telescope for focus and a million watts of power, this test program is an important stage in bringing laser weapons closer to operational status. The key to practicality is the miniaturization of lasers and their power sources to allow them to be placed on small platforms such as aircraft and satellites. Other problems may also be reduced if not eliminated. The British have developed X-ray lasers which would solve the problem of atmospheric interference by using the invisible light spectrum. Jamming of the light-wave frequencies of lasers may be eliminated by the free electron laser which has a continuous wave frequency. Nor are high-energy lasers as potential weapons confined solely to the two superpowers. Many believe that the Japanese high-energy laser program is second only to those of the United States and Soviet Union. The advent of the laser as a major weapon of strategic defense could well alter the strategic balance by making countries such as Japan strategically independent of either superpower by giving them effective defenses against nuclear attack.

Lasers may even prove to be less effective than particle beams as weapons. Lasers direct large amounts of energy in the form of photons (small units of energy with no mass). Particle beams are streams of atomic and subatomic particles – electrons and protons – which strike the target with velocities near the speed of light. Large numbers of them penetrate and transfer energy to the electrons of the target's atoms to create enough heat to melt or crack the target, or at the least fatally affect its electronics. Particle beams are being considered for the same air-, missile- and satellite-defense missions as are strategic lasers. One offensive mission could be to serve in effect as a giant neutron bomb to irradiate hundreds of square miles of earth from space platforms. 'This would destroy a population without breaking a single brick,' said one scientist. Such a death ray from space would have to be far more powerful than the state of particle-beam technology is likely to be able to permit for the foreseeable future.

Workable particle-beam weapons essentially depend on miniaturization of the primary components: an accelerator to speed up the particles, power supply, energy storage, and target-direction, tracking and aiming systems. Particle beams also tend to lose focus in space and are deflected by the earth's magnetic field by amounts which could be as much as one kilometer per 1000 kilometers of range. Countermeasures may also be relatively simple by jamming the weapon's radars and the use of decoy targets and chaff. Like the laser, however, the particle-beam weapon may yet have its engineering problems solved and emerge as a

major addition to the arsenals of the world.

Because of their potential for altering the strategic balance, directed-energy weapons are yet another area of major technological competition between the United States and Soviet Union. Both sides have invested heavily in these technologies. The United States has

Below: the USAF Airborne Laser Laboratory, a modified Boeing NKC-135 aircraft, is a major step toward operational laser weapons.

Bottom: this view of an operator's console in an MPS-11 mobile radar site serves to emphasize the dependence on electronics of modern military organizations.

spent about $1,500,000,000 on laser development alone while the Soviet Union is believed to have invested about 5,000,000,000. The United States has some lead in laser technology but the Soviets are believed to be well ahead in the development of particle-beam technology.

The military significance of these technological developments was formally recognized in 1972 in the Soviet-American Antiballistic Missile Treaty, which forbids the testing or deployment of space-based antiballistic-missile systems or components. The consequences of a space-based antiballistic-missile system on the military relationship between the two superpowers would be so great that some have even suggested one side would resort to military means to prevent the other from deploying its system. With each side probably 10 years or less from operational systems and the treaty due for renewal in 1982, it is entirely possible that the two sides may opt to maintain the status quo in space defense as the safest means of preventing fundamental change in the strategic balance. It is also possible that each side will successfully launch the new space-based technology, in which case the future may hold a transition from the present nuclear-based strategic offenses to laser-based defenses, a development which would make the world a much safer place in which to live.

Directed-energy weapons will also be dependent on the array of computers, sensors, and C^3 hardware which make possible all of modern weaponry. Yet the application of modern electronics to weaponry has brought great increases in performance and capabilities, but not the reductions in cost that the commercial and consumer electronic areas have enjoyed. Calculator prices, for example, have dropped between 10–90 percent but the cost of weapons has been growing at similar rates. Much of this increase results from electronics. Over 40 percent of the cost of the Abrams battle tank lies in its electronic fire-control equipment, while the F-15 fighter has 27 microprocessors, the integrated circuit equivalent of a general purpose computer. One important reason for the staggering increases in the cost of wea-

pons is that electronics are used not to decrease costs but to expand operational performance. The US Army, for example, is considering replacing the laser-guided shell with imaging infra-red Maverick missiles, because the Maverick is considered to have better all-weather capability. The Copperhead costs $10,000, the Maverick about $50,000, but each can kill only one tank.

Apart from its profound impact on military hardware since World War II, science has also strongly affected attitudes and approaches to the conduct of war. In a sense, the application of science to war has come about as both the United States and NATO on one side and the Soviet Union and Warsaw pact on the other firmly believe that a science of war exists. They think that what Jeffrey Record has called 'this most complex, uncontrollable and least understood of all human events' is susceptible to systematic analysis and the tools of modern scientific management. Both sides have tried to reduce the uncertainties surrounding future conflicts through quantitative analysis and simulation using computers and probability theory. The latter theory predicts results in terms of the odds on winning, but it cannot predict the outcomes of specific sequences of events. It requires that assumptions be made about many aspects of both (or all) combatants, but the real assumptions of the enemy can never be known. World War III has already been fought by computers perhaps thousands of times on both sides of the Iron Curtain. This is the only way that each side can measure its strength against the other in various theoretical circumstances.

For all the impressive changes science has wrought in warfare in the postwar period, it has yet to produce the ultimate weapon of Edison and thus make war unthinkable. The PGM, particle beam and laser are not in this category because they bring only temporary advantage to one side until the other side adjusts. It was in fact in World War II that science demonstrated its greatest military power in the atomic bombing of Japan. This is as close as it has yet been able to come to bestowing an ultimate weapon on the world.

The summer of 1945 was a time of fear for the people of Hiroshima. Day after day clouds of B-29 bombers flew past their city of 300,000 on highly destructive incendiary raids against other hapless Japanese cities. The B-29s had become such a common part of daily life that the Japanese called them 'B-san' (Mr B). But the inhabitants of Hiroshima were not unduly concerned when the air-raid sirens sounded early on the morning of 6 August. An American weather aircraft usually flew over about that time and only one aircraft appeared in the sky. That aircraft was a B-29 named *Enola Gay*, lumbering along under the weight of a 9000-pound bomb dubbed 'Little Boy.' When 'Little Boy' was released around 0815 hours, the bomber lifted a good 10 feet, so heavy had been its burden. The awesome explosion which followed drove the stone columns by the entrance of the Shima Clinic straight into the ground, melted cobblestones and sent a hail of broken window glass flying through the city. It also killed or wounded around 80,000 people, including most of the city's doctors and nurses. Three days later, a second bomb – named 'Fat Man' – wrought

Overleaf: part of the devastation caused by the atomic bomb at Nagasaki is viewed by Doctor Nagai, himself a radiation victim.

similar destruction of the city of Nagasaki.

The nuclear devastation of Hiroshima and Nagasaki ushered in a new age. The power demonstrated by the new weapons was so great that it forced a reconsideration of the fundamental questions of strategy and set off an arms race between the United States and the Soviet Union which has resulted in arsenals with so great a destructive potential as to be simply beyond human grasp. The advent of operational nuclear weapons caused statesmen and military men to reexamine the political purposes for which states use their military force and how that force is deployed in war. Diplomacy was also affected because the new destructiveness which had entered warfare made international conflict so potentially dangerous.

The nuclear arms race had in fact begun early in World War II, when the United States and Britain made a major and ultimately successful effort to develop a nuclear weapon before the Germans. Although the Soviet Union began a modest nuclear-weapons development program in 1942, it was only in mid-August 1945 that Stalin called together his chief weapons designers and reportedly said, 'A single demand of you, comrades: provide us with atomic weapons in the shortest possible time. You know that Hiroshima has shaken

the whole world. The equilibrium has been destroyed. Provide the bomb – it will remove a great danger from us.' Four years later the first Soviet nuclear test took place in the Ustyurt Desert. Since that time, the United States and the Soviet Union have been joined in the nuclear club by Britain, France, China and India. There is strong suspicion that Israel and South Africa also have nuclear weapons and that Pakistan is about to reach that goal as well.

The scientific work which made possible the nuclear weapons of 1945 dates from the late nineteenth-century research of the French physicist Henri Becquerel, who identified the nature of radiation in 1896 and discovered electrons the following year. Marie and Pierre Curie isolated the natural elements radium and polonium in 1898. The 1920s saw the basic work in nuclear physics and the early research of the men most associated with the first bomb – Enrico Fermi, Edward Teller, and J Robert Oppenheimer. In December 1941 the United States first harnessed its resources for serious coordinated work on a nuclear bomb in what subsequently became the Manhattan Project under the direction of General Leslie Groves. The early Soviet effort was directed by Igor Kurchatov, Lev Artsimovich and Andrei Sakharov,

the political dissident of the 1970s who is known as the father of the Soviet hydrogen bomb.

Nuclear weapons result from the discovery of the fact that splitting the nucleus of an atom with neutrons releases tremendous energy in a process called fission. Only the heaviest natural elements, such as uranium or the man-made plutonium, will split readily with a relatively small energy input. Each split nucleus of these elements releases about 20,000,000 times as much energy as that involved in the chemical reaction of a TNT explosion. Once atoms begin to split in the nuclear-fission process, they produce more neutrons which in turn split more nuclei and begin a chain reaction. A balanced and controlled chain reaction is the basis for the steady production of nuclear reactors, while a sudden unbalanced reaction produces a nuclear explosion.

Above right: a 'Little Boy' fission bomb of the type used on Hiroshima. Its yield was equivalent to some 12,500 tons of TNT.

Right: the 'Fat Man' bomb detonated over Nagasaki weighed approximately 10,000lb and gave the same yield as 'Little Boy.'

Below: the Hiroshima bomb was dropped by the B-29 Superfortress Enola Gay, *which is pictured during training in New Mexico.*

Left: the atomic burst over Hiroshima shows the column of smoke 20,000ft high and the overpressure spreading from its base.

Above: a series of four photographs taken from the escort B-29 on the Nagasaki mission. The 'Fat Man' bomb detonates over the city, the fireball forms and then the typical mushroom cloud, which rises rapidly skyward.

Right: the mushroom cloud billows over Nagasaki as the Superfortresses withdraw.

Fission weapons have only two basic designs. The 'gun assembly' design is not common and uses a chemical explosive to fire a subcritical bullet of Uranium 235 or Plutonium 239 into another subcritical mass to raise the number of free neutrons to the level required for a chain reaction. The more usual design jackets subcritical mass with conventional explosive. The shock wave produced by the conventional explosion then compresses the nuclear material to the critical point. The explosive power of these weapons is expressed in terms of tons of TNT equivalence. The bombs dropped on Hiroshima and Nagasaki were equivalent in power to 12,500 tons of TNT, or 12.5 kilotons. The power of a nuclear weapon as measured in this fashion is termed the 'yield' of the weapon.

The development of nuclear weapons proceeded rapidly beyond the primitive early fission bombs. By late 1952 the United States had exploded the first hydrogen bomb in the form of a clumsy device weighing 65 tons dubbed 'Mike.' By the following summer, the Soviet Union had duplicated this endeavor. 'H-bombs,' as they were then called, do not use fission but a process called fusion which is not found naturally on earth. Whereas fission splits the nuclei of heavy elements, fusion combines the nuclei of light elements (typically hydrogen to lithium) into heavier nuclei. In the same process that occurs in the sun and stars, the nuclei of hydrogen atoms are banged together so violently that they fuse into helium. The fusion bomb uses the heat produced by a fission trigger to start the fusion process, which is termed thermonuclear because the reaction is sustained by heat rather than neutrons. The fusion process has not yet been harnessed for nonmilitary purposes, although it may well be by the turn of the century. Fusion weapons are considerably more powerful than fission weapons, hence their yields are usually measured in millions of tons of TNT, or megatons. The yield of a one-megaton weapon exceeds the aggregate TNT yield of all the bombs dropped on Germany by the Allies in World War II. The largest nuclear device ever detonated was a 50-megaton bomb exploded by the Soviet Union in 1961. Nothing

approaching that magnitude has since been attempted.

There are a number of significant differences between fission and fusion weapons. The size of fission weapons is limited by the critical mass of their radioactive components, but any amount of the elements of a fusion bomb can be packaged into a weapon without the problem of premature detonation. The materials used in fusion weapons are cheaper and more readily available than the expensive and specially prepared Uranium 235 and Plutonium 239 of fission weapons. The fusion weapon produces less radioactivity, in that its main product is a light radioactive substance in gaseous form called Tritium which mixes into the atmosphere. The other significant product is the 'garbage' from its fission trigger. Thus fusion weapons are said to be 'cleaner' than fission weapons in that they produce smaller amounts of radioactivity in proportion to their yield. The fission and fusion principles can also be combined into what is called the 'fission-fusion-fission' weapon in which a fusion device is jacketed with Uranium 238. This combination adds enormously to the power of the explosion, but also enormously increases the radioactive residue. This can be a very 'dirty' explosion indeed.

The trend of the 1970s, however, has

been toward smaller and cleaner weapons. Marked advances in guidance technologies have allowed the use of smaller warheads. The Soviet SS-9 ICBM, for example, carried a 25-megaton warhead because it might well land several miles from its intended target, while the American Titan ICBM carries a nine-megaton warhead for much the same reason. These early nuclear delivery systems essentially used 1950s technology. In contrast the Minuteman III ICBM, mainstay of the United States strategic forces throughout the 1970s, carries three small warheads of 170 kilotons apiece, but can drop those warheads within 1000 feet or so of their intended targets. Other guidance technologies now enable smaller missiles, such as cruise missiles and short-range ballistic missiles, to have almost pinpoint accuracies and thus obviate the need for blockbuster warheads. The ICBMs of the 1980s, such as the US MX ICBM and several Soviet ICBMs known to be under development, are also expected to come close to such accuracies.

There is much current interest in and controversy about, neutron or enhanced-radiation weapons. These small

Below: Hiroshima survivors are treated for severe burns. Such injuries will be the primary cause of deaths in urban areas.

fusion devices limit yield, but produce large amounts of prompt, penetrating radiation. They are thus the equal in radiation 'kill' to a much larger fission warhead, but produce much less physical destruction and radioactive garbage. Their rationale has been for use against large Soviet armored formations in the highly urbanized mileu of Central Europe, where the level of collateral damage is a very real concern. Owing to their antipersonnel orientation, enhanced-radiation warheads are fraught with political and emotional overtones and have yet to enter the arsenal of any country. The United States and France are both developing enhanced-radiation weapons, but have deferred decision on production. Neutron weapons are believed by observers of the Soviet forces to be well within their capability as well.

When a nuclear explosion occurs, the energy is generated very rapidly in a small volume. The warhead components are vaporized and an ultrahot, rapidly expanding fireball is created. Nuclear explosions release several kinds of energy: kinetic (blast), thermal (heat), prompt radiation, delayed radiation (fallout) and electromagnetic pulse. Approximately half of the energy takes the form of blast with the same, albeit enormously magnified, destructive effects as a chemical explosion. Blast is a shock wave, literally a wall of compressed air, moving away from 'ground zero' at supersonic speed. The pressure from the blast crushes structures as it passes and is termed overpressure. Overpressure is calculated in pounds per square inch (psi). Any structure not specifically reinforced, (or 'hardened,') will generally be destroyed by a minimum of 5psi, which would place about 180 tons of force on a two-story house wall.

Strong winds, termed the dynamic pressure, follow the shock wave. An explosion creating 5psi of overpressure

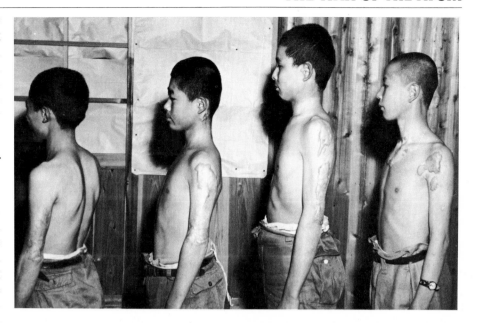

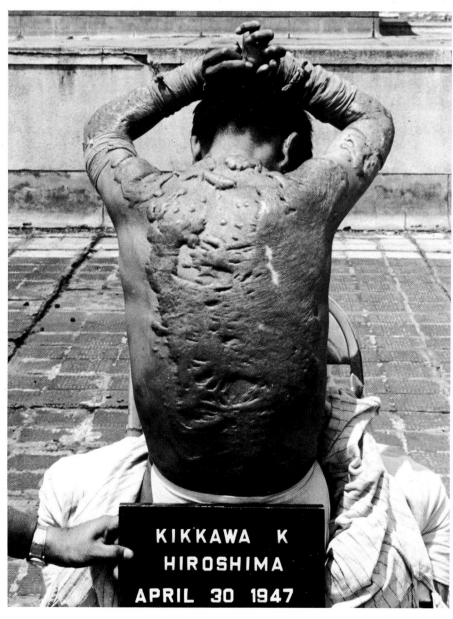

Above right: the scars on four Hiroshima schoolboys were caused by flash burns. The psychological scars are just as severe.

Right: another Hiroshima survivor displays the keloid tumors that he developed as a result of flash burns.

KIKKAWA K
HIROSHIMA
APRIL 30 1947

will also create winds of 160 miles per hour, while winds of 290 miles per hour are associated with 10psi explosions. Structures generally are destroyed by overpressure. People are able to withstand up to 30psi, but they are in danger from dynamic pressure, which makes twigs, pebbles, broken glass and other small objects as deadly as shrapnel and can also hurl people against hard surfaces with lethal results. Deaths associated with overpressure generally result from the collapse of occupied buildings.

Nuclear weapons can employ either ground or air bursts. Ground bursts produce very high overpressure in a very limited area and also produce a crater. When delivered very accurately, a ground burst is the most efficient means of destroying a small point target such as a missile silo or hardened command post. The disadvantages are that such bursts create a considerable amount of immediate, local fallout and that nuclear weapons, at least until very recently, were seldom able to be delivered with the necessary accuracy. An air burst will distribute a lesser amount of overpressure over a considerably wider area, which can be controlled by varying the height of the burst. Air bursts usually create no crater and little immediate fallout.

A nuclear explosion releases over a third of its energy as heat and infrared light which is radiated in less than a minute. The heat and flash precede the blast wave by seconds and can cause some minutes of complete flash blindness as far as 13 miles from a one-megaton explosion. Thermal effects are highly dangerous to people. A one-megaton explosion will cause third degree burns (meaning skin tissue is destroyed) up to five miles away, second degree burns (blisters) at about six miles, and first degree burns (equivalent to severe sunburn) at about seven miles, Third degree burns over a quarter of the body or second degree over a third will probably cause death without immediate and specialized medical care.

Almost two-thirds of the deaths at Hiroshima on the first day after the explosion resulted from severe burns. Owing to the clear warm weather, many people were outdoors in light clothing and thus unprotected. John Hersey described the result in his book *Hiroshima*: '. . . their faces were wholly burned, their eye sockets were hollow, the fluid from their melted eyes had run down their cheeks.'

The thermal output of a nuclear explosion usually has strong incendiary effects as well. It has been calculated that the incendiary effects of 'Little Boy' on Hiroshima were equal to 1000 tons of incendiary bombs. Unprotected flammable materials will ignite directly, while other fires result from ruptured gas lines and oil tanks, damaged electric circuitry, furnaces and stoves. The Japanese cities were particularly vulnerable to fire, because of their high density of wooden structures. American, Soviet and European cities would be much less vulnerable in this respect, because of their propensity for concrete construction. The water main at Hiroshima also ruptured, 70 percent of the fire equipment was destroyed by the collapse of fire stations, and most of the fire personnel were unable to report. About 20 minutes after the explosion, a large firestorm developed, fuelled by a strong wind, and six hours later it had completed the destruction of over four square miles of the city. Such firestorms are not unique to nuclear explosions, however, as the intense conventional bombing of Hamburg and Dresden caused firestorms of virtually the same magnitude. The hilly terrain of Nagasaki apparently spared it the added horror of a firestorm, although the city did experience extensive fires. The thermal effects of a nuclear explosion can be distinctly mitigated by such factors as rain or fog, dust, or hilly terrain, or enhanced by low-lying white clouds and clean air.

About five percent of the energy of a nuclear weapon is released as direct or 'prompt' radiation in the form of gamma rays, neutrons and beta particles. Gamma rays are a highly penetrating form of X-rays which do serious damage to the human body. Beta particles and neutrons have short range, but cause severe burns in large doses. Major uncertainties still surround the effects of radiation on people, because the data stem mainly from studies of the Hiroshima and Nagasaki victims, and a few subsequent isolated incidents involving humans and laboratory work with animals. Death from radiation sickness, however, is most unpleasant. The standard United States government manual on nuclear weapons effects describes it in these terms: 'The initial symptoms are . . . nausea, vomiting, diarrhea, loss of appetite and malaise.' After two to three weeks, 'there is a tendency to bleed into various organs, and small hemorrhages under the skin . . . are observed,' along with loss of hair and ulceration around the lips which may spread through the entire gastrointestinal tract. Eventually 'the decrease in the white cells of the blood and injury to other immune mechanisms of the body . . . allow an overwhelming infection to develop.

Current US Army radiation casualty criteria include three general categories of human response to prompt radiation. The central nervous syndrome results from doses of 2000 rads (unit of absorbed radiation roughly equal to a roentgen) or more. The symptoms usually appear within minutes of exposure and range from apathy and drowsiness to convulsions and collapse. A dose of 5000 rads or more will physically incapacitate within five minutes of exposure and cause death within two days. The gastrointestinal syndrome results from 500 or more rads, with symptoms ranging from loss of appetite and vomiting to severe diarrhea, high fever and coma within three to five days of exposure. Exposure to 1000 rads causes death in roughly two weeks. The hematopoietic syndrome is associated with 100 rads or more. Symptoms are fatigue, headaches, chills and fever. Death may come in three to four weeks, but exposures of less than 200 rads will cause few deaths.

At burst heights of 500–1500 feet, both a 10-kiloton fission weapon and a one-kiloton enhanced-radiation weapon will produce 8000 rads out to half a mile and 650 rads out to less than a mile. Such radiation, especially from enhanced radiation weapons, would be a prime cause of fatalities among forces on a nuclear battlefield. Few urban dwellers in a nuclear attack would be exposed to such dosages, because they

are more likely to be killed by blast or thermal effects. Those that were so exposed, however, would have an estimated 90 percent chance of fatal illness from 600 rads.

Civilians would be far more at risk from the delayed radiation known as fallout. Surface or near-surface bursts scoop up and make radioactive large amounts of ordinary materials such as soil. The fireball of a one-megaton bomb will rise rapidly until it enters the stratosphere about six to eight miles above the earth. It then stabilizes and spreads over an area as large as four miles in diameter. Depending on wind patterns, the fallout area may be 100–200 miles long and 25 miles wide with a settling time of roughly eight hours. Local fallout can cause a high rate of fatality. The 15-megaton fusion device detonated over Bikini Atoll in 1954 produced a fallout pattern that affected people 100 miles downwind, who suffered severe short- and long-term radiation effects, while fishermen 80 miles away received radiation doses that ultimately killed one of them.

There are also long-range and long-term effects of fallout. Radioactive materials such as Strontium 90, Cesium 137, Iodine 131 and Carbon 14 have long active lives and can enter the food chains halfway round the world. Recognition of these effects from the active atmospheric testing from the mid-1940s to the early 1960s led to a ban on such testing in 1963 which has been observed by most of the nuclear club. Traces of fallout from the American and Soviet tests of that period can still be detected, while Strontium 90 from a Chinese atmospheric test in the summer of 1980 was found in the food chain of California several months later.

All of the symptoms discussed so far can occur in combinations to cause

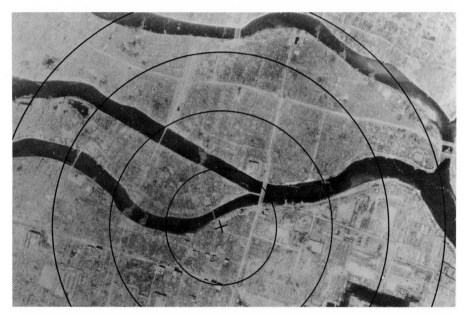

Top right: Hiroshima ground zero (the point immediately below the explosion) photographed before the attack.

Above right: ground zero viewed after the attack, with concentric circles marked at 1000-foot intervals.

Right: the port of Nagasaki was photographed by a reconnaissance aircraft immediately after the explosion on 9 August 1945.

fatalities. A person suffering from non-lethal injuries from blast, who also receives a nonlethal dose of radiation, may succumb from the combination. This is because, for example, radiation damage to the blood will raise the victim's susceptibility to blood loss and infection. Such compounding of injuries seems likely to raise the toll of civilian fatalities substantially in a nuclear attack.

Nuclear explosions produce one last noteworthy effect. The absorption of gamma rays into the air or ground creates secondary reactions, which in turn produce electromagnetic waves similar to radio waves but many thousands of times stronger. This phenomenon, known as electromagnetic pulse (EMP), is literally a single pulse lasting but a fraction of a second. Ground bursts produce very strong EMP at very short ranges, while air bursts cause much less and the ranges are still very limited. However a very high air burst, at an altitude of 19 miles or above, will produce extremely powerful EMP with ranges of thousands of miles and great potential for serious damage to electronics. A major nuclear attack will undoubtedly feature a few very high altitude bursts intended to damage and disrupt communications and electric power systems. One burst at around 90 miles altitude would blanket the central third of the United States, with strong EMP effects, while a burst at 450 miles would more than cover the entire country.

As far as has yet been determined, EMP is not a threat to people, nor has it yet been determined to what extent telephone systems may be affected. What is not in doubt are the serious effects on radio, radar, and electronics in general. The passage of radio and radar waves is affected for periods of minutes or hours. This 'nuclear blackout' has serious implications for both attacker and defender. Electronic facilities such as radar stations and communications centers can be penetrated by EMP through wave guides, antennas, cabling, power lines, grounding systems and even sewer systems and unshielded walls. EMP can literally burn out electronic components or cause functional and operational up-

sets. In general, the more advanced the electronics, the more vulnerable they are to EMP damage. Modern integrated solid-state circuitry is, for example, 10,000,000 times more vulnerable than old-fashioned vacuum tubes.

EMP, which can also be generated by nonnuclear means, is forcing complex and expensive protection measures to be incorporated in the design of military electronics systems. These protective steps are called 'hardening,' as are the steps to reinforce physical facilities against overpressure. If a general nuclear war broke out, however, it is very much an open question as to how much of the electronics systems, both military and civilian, on which the United States and USSR depend would survive the detonation of the tens of thousands of warheads targeted on each country by the other.

The only nuclear weapons ever used in war were the relatively small bombs dropped on Hiroshima and Nagasaki. Yet a number of studies have used the nuclear weapons effects described above to calculate the result of a major nuclear attack on an urban center. The most recent exercise, published by the Office of Technology Assessment of the US Congress in 1979, examined theoretical attacks on Detroit and Leningrad. A one-megaton surface burst with downtown Detroit as ground zero would dig a crater 200 feet deep and 1000 feet across surrounded by several hundred more feet of highly radioactive soil. Virtually all structures would be destroyed out to 1.7 miles from ground zero and out to 2.7 miles multistory concrete buildings would probably be reduced to skeletal structures and houses would be demolished.

About half of the 250,000 population of this area would be killed, mostly from collapsing buildings, and most of the remainder injured. Prompt radiation would not be a significant factor, since most people in its lethal area would be killed by blast effects. Many fires would start but a firestorm would be unlikely. Beyond 2.7 miles injuries would be high but deaths probably only about five percent. Damage would be

less complete but still extensive. People unprotected from local fallout might receive 300-rad doses in the first hour. Total casualties are estimated at 650,000 with 220,000 fatalities. A one-megaton air burst with its more extensive area of effects would cause over 1,000,000 casualties among Detroit's population of 4,300,000. A one-megaton air burst

Right: the center of Hiroshima was obliterated by the atomic bomb, but the harder, concrete structures were more resistant to overpressure.

over Leningrad would cause similar damage levels, but about twice as many casualties because of the higher population density of that city.

Rather than one large weapon aimed at the center of a major urban area, a more likely targeting strategy is to release a pattern of warheads aimed at destroying specific military and in-dustrial objectives. One recent study postulated 10 one-megaton warheads targeted on military and industrial facilities in the Boston area. The com-bined detonations would produce five psi of overpressure over more than 500 square miles, kill 1,500,000 people from prompt blast and thermal effects, destroy 80 percent of the area's in-dustrial capacity and cause extensive fire damage.

When an attack is made against purely military objectives on a national scale a similar pattern occurs. For ex-ample there are nine ICBM fields in the American Midwest where they are based. A Soviet attack aimed only at these specific installations in a missile

duel would bathe much of the Midwest in a zone of lethal radiation. It would also create a huge fallout area which could reach parts of the east coast. When the additional purely military targets that the Soviet Union might be expected to attack are considered, such as bomber and submarine bases and communications facilities, most of the United States is seen to be at risk. The same conclusion applies to the Soviet Union in the event of an American attack aimed solely at military objectives. Even if both sides avoid targeting each other's cities, there will

Left and below: general views of Hiroshima show the devastation wrought by the atomic bombing near ground zero.

still be horrendous civilian casualties from fallout and radiation effects.

Both countries have maintained civil defense programs against the contingency of nuclear attack since the 1950s. The early United States program concentrated on urban evacuation, but then switched toward urban shelters against blast and fallout. Since the mid-1970s the focus has again switched to evacuation, under the assumption that enough warning would be available to make this feasible. In recent years the civil-defense program has been, in the words of a 1979 Congressional study, 'marked by vacillation, shifts in direction, and endless reorganization.' The same study concludes that while civil defense looks effective on paper, 'no

one at all thinks that the United States has an effective civil defense.' Critics claim that the program is harmful beyond its ineffectiveness, in that its very existence creates the illusion that the effects of nuclear war can be mitigated. The official position is that it would be 'totally irresponsible to make no preparation at all.'

In contrast to the United States, the USSR has mounted a consistent long-term effort in civil defense. An unclassified CIA study released in 1978 stated that Soviet goals are to protect the political and administrative leadership, essential workers, and the general populace in that order, and to protect productivity and prepare for economic recovery. The Soviets have an extensive

shelter program but rely heavily on evacuation. There is also a program to harden industrial facilities. Commenting on Soviet prospects for economic recovery, however, the CIA study notes '. . . the coordination of requirements with available supplies and transportation is a complex problem for Soviet planners even in peacetime, let alone following a large-scale nuclear attack.' The contribution of the Soviet civil-defense program to Soviet ability to cope with general nuclear war has been a subject of continuing controversy within the United States defense community. Some claim that it would make a significant difference in Soviet ability to endure a war, while others argue that the Soviet effort holds little

more promise of effectiveness than that of the United States.

There are currently around 50,000 warheads of assorted sizes in the arsenals of the nuclear powers. Use of even 500 of these warheads in a general nuclear war would probably kill some 50,000,000 people and leave 25,000,000 more with some degree of radiation sickness. Roughly half of all Americans and Soviets would die and the population of Europe would be decimated as well. Civil defense would have little effect on the number of casualties and medical assistance would be virtually nonexistent. Epidemics of diseases such as cholera and typhus are considered almost certain in the aftermath, as normal water and sewage systems would be disrupted and large numbers of people made homeless. Longer term effects would be a greatly increased incidence of cancer and genetic damage.

Possibly the most serious, but certainly the least understood, problem arising from nuclear warfare in the short run would be changes in the climate, due to destruction of much of the earth's ozone layer and the injection of large amounts of dust into the stratosphere. The heat of the explosions would create large amounts of nitrogen oxides, which aid in the conversion of ozone into oxygen. The ozone layer, the outer reach of the stratosphere

Top: American soldiers examine the effects of the blast from the Hiroshima bomb on steel and concrete structures.

Above: this apartment over half a mile from ground zero remained standing because its large window area allowed the blast to pass through.

about 20 miles from the earth's surface, normally protects people, plants and animals from the ultraviolet radiation of the sun. Increased ultraviolet radiation could seriously affect crop raising and animal husbandry and even cause cases of fatal sunburn. However, the ozone layer would in time regenerate itself.

Hundreds of large nuclear explosions would pump thousands of tons of dust into the upper atmosphere. This would affect the amount of sunlight reaching the earth and alter the weather. A global cooling of one degree Fahrenheit would, for example, eliminate all wheat growing in Canada. A growing body of scientific opinion, however, now believes that the dust factor might not be all that significant, but rather similar to major volcanic events such as Krakatoa in 1883 and Mount St Helens in 1980.

Nuclear war also has demonstrable psychological and spiritual dimensions. In his study of the survivors of Hiroshima and Nagasaki, Robert J Lifton identified one aspect of the nuclear experience as the breakdown of the 'line between life and death,' or 'confusion over who was alive and who was dead.' One survivor remembered thinking 'It doesn't matter if I die . . . this is the end of Hiroshima, of Japan, of human kind,' while another said simply

'It is as if I were already dead.' Nikita Krushchev is remembered for his remark that in nuclear war 'the survivors would envy the dead,' but Lifton's studies indicate that psychologically and spiritually the survivors would be among the dead. Beyond their experience of a personal apocalypse, the survivors had a strong sense of all life being extinguished, that the effects of the bomb continued indefinitely and lethally in the form of grotesque symptoms – leukemia, cancers, genetic effects – that left them tainted with deformity and death. 'A single small weapon has created a totality of destruction,' concludes Lifton. 'There is unending lethal influence, a sense of being a victim of a force that threatens the species, that reverberates psychologically on these people.'

The most far-reaching yet unfathomable effects of nuclear war may well lie in the socio-political arena. Mankind has endured any number of horrendous

disasters in the course of recorded history. There was, for example, the Black Death in the fourteenth century, up to 100,000,000 dead during the great mid-nineteenth century rebellions of Imperial China, the mind-boggling slaughter on the Western Front in World War I (250,000 French and Germans dead at Verdun, 60,000 British dead in the first hour of the Somme), and an estimated 20,000,000 dead in the Soviet Union alone in World War II. Yet Lifton's studies strongly suggest that, whatever else they can endure, people respond differently to nuclear war. The popular response to the Black Death, also a unique experience in history, suggests that seemingly arbitrary, grotesque death inflicted by invisible agents (whether microbes or radiation) on a large scale considerably weakens popular willingness to acquiesce to accepted or mandated conventions and responsibilities. As Henry Kissinger, one of the early students of nuclear matters, wrote, 'No one knows how governments or people will react to a nuclear explosion under conditions where both sides possess vast arsenals.' At the least seriously demoralized, but perhaps also suffering from the 'alive or dead' disorientation characterizing the Hiroshima and Nagasaki survivors, people may simply refuse to acknowledge or cooperate

Below: the demolished Mitsubishi torpedo plant, once the largest factory of its kind, photographed a year after the attack.

with the duly constituted authorities, if indeed those authorities are not themselves so affected.

The disruption of those 'intensely interdependent components that enable a modern society to function' might well cause government in the United States, Soviet Union and Europe to disintegrate into local and regional units, at least for a time. The industrial societies might revert to pre-1900 standards of living. The Soviet Union in particular might find it difficult to reintegrate its sizable non-Russian populations and be forced into military action to reconstitute its rule in certain areas.

At least some of those who worked on the first bomb had intimations of these ultimate consequences of nuclear weapons. 'There were many of us who really wished we couldn't do it, that it wasn't possible,' said a Manhattan Project worker. J Robert Oppenheimer, the father of the American bomb, said in 1948 that 'In some sort of crude sense, which no vulgarity, no humor, no overstatement can quite extinguish, the physicists have known sin, and this is a knowledge which they cannot lose.' Clearly 'the bomb' touches on Christian fascination with punishment and retribution in the form of calamity and thus provides modern Western man with his vision of apocalypse in the form of a nuclear holocaust.

Although the Western military establishment, and one suspects the Soviet armed forces as well, tends to plan its use of nuclear weapons as though these are simply vastly more effective conventional weapons, the political leaders of the two blocs appear to have been suitably awed by the power that has been rendered to them. Neither side views nuclear war as a rational instrument of policy, nor is either at all sanguine about the outcome.

The United States has built much of its military policy around the deterrent

Right: a dissipating atomic cloud dwarfs troops observing an atomic explosion during the heyday of US nuclear weapons' testing in 1951.

Far right: the first color photograph of an atomic explosion, taken from a distance of 10 miles in New Mexico, 1946.

effect of its nuclear arsenal. Since the early 1950s, 'prevention by threat' has been the chief purpose of the American nuclear arsenal. As one student of the subject has said, 'The whole basis of deterrence is: you make things good by making them possibly awful.' In the 1950s, United States policy was 'massive retaliation' – aggression by the Soviet Union would unleash the United States nuclear arsenal. The threat of American nuclear power, it was thought, held back the huge conventional forces of the Soviet Union. By the early 1960s United States Secretary of Defense Robert MacNamara and his associates had concluded that there was no way to fight a nuclear war, 'because there was no way to be certain of keeping such a war from inflicting destruction on a catastrophic scale.' They thus devised the nuclear doctrine of 'mutual assured destruction' (MAD), which held that both sides were deterred by the prospect of Armageddon. An attack by one would cause retaliation by the other and both would be destroyed. This conception of deterrence through mutual vulnerability soon came to be known as the 'delicate balance of terror.' Succeeding administrations have followed the broad outlines of MacNamara's nuclear weapons policy.

Like the United States, the Soviet Union has a well-justified concern about nuclear war and its consequences. Initially, Stalin refused to come to grips with the implications of nuclear weapons for war and politics. He continued to insist that the basis of victory in war was still a superior sociopolitical system, hence Soviet victory was ultimately assured. After Stalin's death in 1953, a strong debate over the significance of nuclear weapons developed and a more flexible view finally emerged under Nikita Khrushchev in the late 1950s. While stating that the Soviet Union would always be in the front ranks of all revolutionary

wars, Khrushchev rejected general nuclear war and local politico-military confrontations capable of growing into such a conflict. He instead espoused 'peaceful coexistence,' which meant staging an economic, ideological and social struggle against the capitalist camp rather than seeking victory through actual warfare.

Under Khrushchev's successor, Leonid Brezhnev, the Soviet politico-military leadership seems to have moved toward a more balanced view of future warfare. While still stressing the calamitous consequences of nuclear war, the Soviets now accept it as a distinct possibility and believe they must be prepared for all military contingencies whether conventional or nuclear. For the Soviets, deterrence stems not from MacNamara's 'delicate balance of terror,' but from powerful and well-balanced forces ready to fight in all conceivable situations.

Both sides have in fact been quietly moving away from earlier conceptions of nuclear war as an unrestrained global holocaust. Rather than a massive nuclear exchange, for example, the United States formalized a decade of movement toward selective and flexible strategic targeting in Presidential Directive 59 of 1980. For the first time, this document admitted that American doctrine was not solely committed to MAD and the targeting of Soviet cities,

Left: tens of thousands of tons of water are lifted skyward by the power of an early underwater explosion at Bikini Atoll in 1946.

Right: a fission explosion rises high over Bikini Atoll in 1946 as part of the active postwar development of nuclear weapons by the US.

but that selective military targeting and limited nuclear war were also options. The Soviet Union has always been disparaging about MAD, but until recently it lacked the force sophistication to contemplate anything other than a mass attack. The advent of sophisticated new ICBMs in recent years now allows the Soviet Union the same flexible options as the United States.

The threat of nuclear war has also become an important part of the political relationship between the United States and USSR over the last decade. The 1963 ban on atmospheric testing was followed in 1974 by a ban on underground tests of weapons over 150 kilotons in yield, because at this level natural and man-made seismic events are easily distinguishable. Formal negotiations, called the Strategic Arms Limitation Talks (SALT), to limit the nuclear arms race and reduce the risk of nuclear war began in 1969 and by mid-1972 had produced three treaties and an interim agreement. After seven more years of hard bargaining over extremely complex issues, a treaty was signed in 1979 to replace the interim agreement. The long duration of the negotiating process, however, has caused this treaty to be overtaken by the march of events and it will probably never enter into force, although nuclear arms talks are continuing among the United States, USSR and other parties.

By the late 1970s a steady Soviet buildup in nuclear arms had enabled the Soviets to eliminate the nuclear superiority enjoyed by the United States since 1945. It is generally agreed that the Soviets will gain a certain nuclear edge over the United States in the 1980s. Having done little with its strategic nuclear arsenal for over a decade, in the late 1970s the United States began a major strategic-arms buildup, along with its first major nuclear-warhead building program in two decades. The warhead program is, however, beset with problems as American nuclear-weapon production facilities desperately need modernizing and expanding – a number still use some equipment dating from the Manhat-

Below: the first tactical nuclear weapon was the US Army's 280mm atomic cannon, seen here during its initial test in 1953.

tan Project – and must compete for limited supplies of nuclear material with the civilian nuclear-power industry. A major modernization and expansion program is planned for the seven nuclear production facilities over the next 10 years, which will serve the needs of the United States well into the next century.

While the issues associated with nuclear-arms limitations have always been contentious in the extreme, both sides were able to reach early agreement on the manifest dangers of nuclear testing. Yet the ban on atmospheric testing has meant that no actual data on nuclear weapons, effects have been gathered since 1963. The underground limit of 150 kilotons means that new warhead designs over that limit cannot

Above: a nuclear test photographed from a height of approximately 12,000ft at a distance of 50 miles from the detonation site.

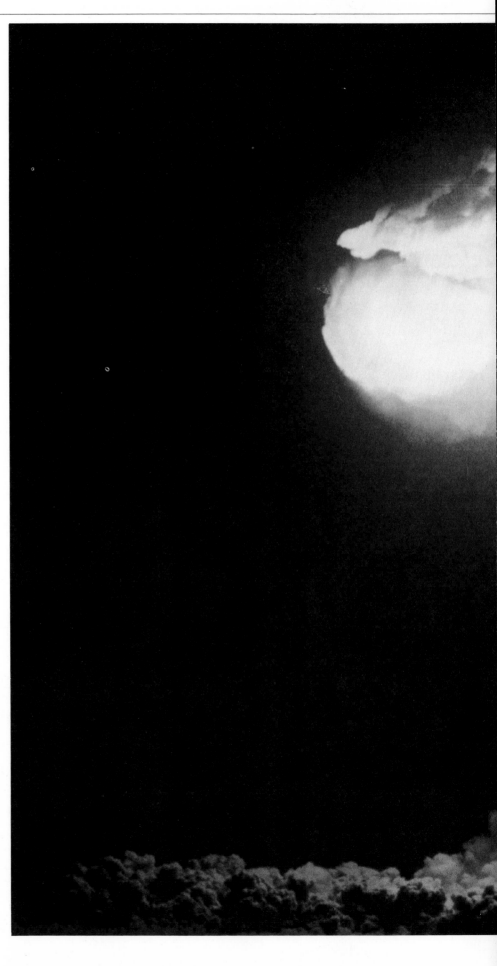

Right: tactical nuclear weapons (for battlefield use) grew out of smaller tests such as this one at Nevada Proving Grounds.

be operationally tested, but must be mathematically projected from smaller designs. This has been noted as a critical point which bears directly on the warhead reliability of each side's arsenal. How much reliance can be placed on weapons that have never been test fired? This could help explain each side's trend toward smaller warheads.

It is generally conceded that World War III has not yet occurred largely because of the existence of nuclear weapons and the uncertainties about the military and political consequences of their use. They have so thoroughly transformed warfare that both sides have sought ways to mitigate or even deny their impact. Prior to the nuclear age, many barriers limited the inherent violence of war: the low levels of weapons effectiveness, the great length of time required for military operations, economic and productive factors and not least the political controls placed on the use of force. Nuclear weapons now bring instantaneous destruction on an almost incalculable scale. For this reason both sides have discovered that nuclear weapons tend to lack credibility as weapons and limit strategic and tactical choice in warfare.

During the 1970s there was a renewal of interest in conventional warfare by both NATO and the Warsaw Pact, amounting to a highly tentative but voluntary limitation on the parameters of war. If major war should break out, no one can predict if or when nuclear weapons would be employed but all fervently hope that that moment will never arrive. The problem is that both sides remain absolutely convinced that the other would resort to its nuclear arsenal if it was losing badly enough, because total defeat cannot be contemplated. World War III may well begin as a conventional conflict, but the key moment will be when the so-called 'nuclear threshold' is reached, the point at which one of the antagonists perceives the imperative to 'go nuclear.' And there are few who doubt that sooner or later that fateful moment will arrive.

'I wish to make an announcement,' Walter Sullivan of the *New York Times* told some 50-odd scientists assembled at the Soviet Embassy in Washington at a cocktail party for the International Geophysical Year rocket and satellite conference. 'I am informed that a satellite is in orbit at an elevation of 900 kilometers. I wish to congratulate our Soviet colleagues on their achievement.' The night was 4 October 1957 and the satellite was *Sputnik I*. This tiny dot of light faintly travelling across the sky (Sputnik means a 'fellow traveller') surprised the world and became the object of a major Soviet propaganda campaign to demonstrate the advanced state of Soviet technology. Sputnik severely embarrassed the United States by challenging its image of technological dominance. The chagrin was especially strong in American space circles because Dr Werner von Braun, one of the leading prizes in the United States' share of the German rocket scientists of World War II, had been

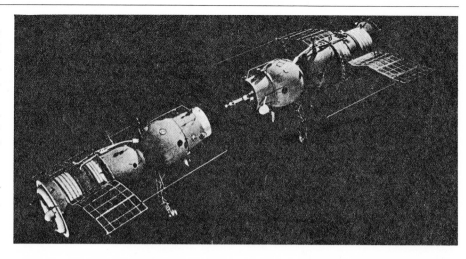

Overleaf: the spacecraft Gemini VII was photographed from Gemini VI during rendezvous and station-keeping maneuvers in December 1965.

Below: the Soviet Union's giant Vostok space booster was derived from the SS-6 intercontinental ballistic missile.

denied permission to launch a satellite over a year before Sputnik. As a result, the first American satellite, *Explorer I*, was not put into orbit until 31 January 1958.

Sputnik not only surprised Americans, it also frightened them because of its clear demonstration of Soviet technological prowess and determination. Sputnik launched the cold war into space and with it the military competition of the Soviet Union and the United States.

An American response was to pour money into building up the educational base of the country, through the National Defense Education Act of 1958, to meet the Soviet technological

Above: two Soviet Soyuz spacecraft prepare to carry out a docking maneuver after making a rendezvous in space in 1969.

challenge. Another was to deprecate the undeniable military significance of Sputnik and to try to place a civilian focus on the United States' space effort. After Sputnik it was clear that rockets which could launch satellites could also launch bombs over great distances and that, as the Democratic Advisory Council stated, 'control of outer space would be a military fact of the highest importance.' But both President Eisenhower and Secretary of Defense Charles Wilson assured the American people that, as Wilson put it, 'Nobody is going to drop anything down on you from a satellite while you are asleep, so don't worry about it.'

And, although orbiting atomic bombs and satellites raining destruction on the world had captured the popular imagination, the President and his secretary were right. The space programs of the United States and Soviet Union quickly developed military aspects, but these have not yet resulted in the deployment of offensive or defensive weapons in space. Instead both sides quickly developed the strategic offensive potential inherent in the marriage of the nuclear warhead and the

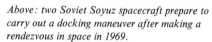

Above right: photographic-intelligence analysis from aerial platforms has become a fine art. This photograph of a Soviet SS-5 missile site was taken during the Cuban missile crisis.

Right: the Cuban port of Mariel.

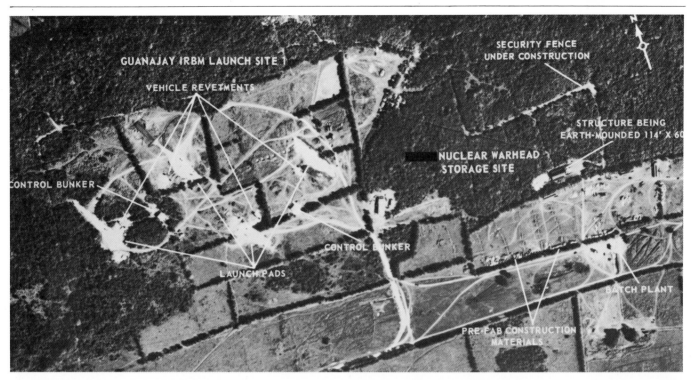

GUANAJAY IRBM LAUNCH SITE 1

VEHICLE REVETMENTS

SECURITY FENCE
UNDER CONSTRUCTION

STRUCTURE BEING
EARTH-MOUNDED 114' X 60

NUCLEAR WARHEAD
STORAGE SITE

CONTROL BUNKER

CONTROL BUNKER

LAUNCH PADS

BATCH PLANT

PRE-FAB CONSTRUCTION
MATERIALS

5 NOVEMBER 1962
MARIEL PORT

6 MISSILE TRANSPORTERS

ERECTOR

3 MISSILE TRANSPORTERS

OXIDIZER TRAILERS

MISSILE TRANSPORTERS

IRBM
PROPELLANT TRAILERS

OXIDIZER TRAILERS

before this decade is out, of landing a man on the moon and returning him safely to earth.' The first man in space was the Soviet Yuri Gagarin in 1961, but the United States did indeed place Neil Armstrong in *Apollo 8* on the moon on 20 July 1969. Before and after this most outstanding (and televised) of space spectaculars, both countries staged a series of heavily publicized space events in impressive demonstra-

Below: astronaut John H Glenn, the first American to orbit the earth, is shown in the Friendship 7 *capsule on 20 February 1962.*

Bottom: a view of the Atlantic Ocean taken by Glenn during his third orbit around the earth, with scattered cloud in the foreground.

Above: a USAF Atlas booster, its tanks empty and rockets dead, drifts away from the reentry section 650 miles above the Atlantic.

long-range ballistic missile to create strategic-bombardment capabilities far beyond the wildest dreams of the early advocates of strategic air power. The military uses of space to date have not been weapon oriented. Instead they have involved the development of communications, warning, and reconnaissance capabilities, which have brought new dimensions to command and control and to military and economic intelligence.

Until recent years the United States was reluctant to admit the military implications of space and consciously limited the military role in favor of the civilian. The National Aeronautics and Space Act of 1958 created the National Aeronautics and Space Administration (NASA) and vested it with overall responsibility for space operations. The new agency was purposely created to prevent the Department of Defense, and especially the Strategic Air Command, from gaining primary responsibility for space. In 1961 President Kennedy confirmed the civilian orientation of the US program in a speech to Congress, 'I believe this nation should commit itself to achieving the goal,

Left: a Delta 131 booster is launched from Cape Canaveral, Florida, with the GOES-2 satellite aboard.

Left: Soviet cosmonauts V Lyakov and V Ryumin remained in space from 25 February until 19 August 1979 during the Salyut 6 mission.

tions of their technological competence and confidence.

The Soviet Union saw space as one way to redress the strategic advantage enjoyed by the United States and its allies from their many bases ringing the USSR. Another similarly motivated program was the unsuccessful attempt in 1962 to use Cuba as a base for medium- and intermediate-range missiles, which the Soviet share of the German rocket scientists had been instrumental in developing in the 1950s. Nikita Khrushchev, the chief architect of the Cuban missile fiasco, illustrated the early Soviet approach to space when he stated in 1961 that 'We placed Gagarin and Titov in space, and we can replace them with bombs which can be diverted to any place on earth.' The strategic concern inherent in this revealing statement, however, was met within a few years by the development of the Soviet ICBM force. The Soviets did use one variant of their large SS-9 ICBM to experiment with a fractional orbital bombardment system (FOBS) in the late 1960s and consistently rejected American proposals to prohibit bombs in orbit unless the United States foreign bases were removed. In 1967, however, the Soviet Union joined the United States in signing the United Nations-sponsored Treaty on the Peaceful Uses of Outer Space, which prohibited the testing and deployment of weapons in space. It seems likely that a combination of the immense technical difficulties of developing space-based

Left: Soviet cosmonauts V Lyakov and V Ryumin remained in space from 25 February until 19 August 1979 during the Salyut 6 mission.

weapons and success in fielding land- and sea-based strategic nuclear weapons motivated the Soviets to foreclose any possibility that the United States might be able to exploit successfully the offensive potential of space and thus gain a renewed strategic advantage.

The armed forces of both sides depend heavily on their satellites for a variety of vital missions, a dependence which is rapidly increasing. These systems, which have become so central in such a short time, consist of the satellite itself, the command and control facilities, launch facilities, and ground-support facilities. The satellite has a

power source, a system for attitude and functional control, and communications systems for contact with its ground stations. In most satellites power comes from solar cells, which can be mounted directly on the body of the satellite or on extended panels. Rechargeable (usually nickel-cadmium) batteries keep the satellite functioning when it is out of direct sunlight. Satellites can, however, carry nuclear power sources, as do long distance space probes. *Cosmos 954*, a five-ton Soviet surveillance satellite which broke up over the Canadian Arctic in January 1978, was powered by 100 pounds of enriched uranium, much to the consternation of the Canadian Government.

The satellite must maintain a specific

orientation (attitude control) to the earth to accomplish its mission. The body of the satellite has small liquid-burning (usually hydrazine) jets, which are managed by the onboard computer. All functions of the satellite, including its communications links to the ground, are managed by this computer. The early satellites had limited lives, but since the early 1970s satellites have stayed aloft for lengthy periods, some as long as several years. Most satellites are in relatively low elliptical orbits and thus pass through the atmosphere and the atmospheric drag from the lower passes distorts the orbit, which periodically needs to be adjusted.

Satellites have varying orbits. Some operate from orbits as low as 80–100 miles above the earth, while one US military satellite in the planning stage will be in orbit 130,000 miles high. A satellite orbit can be in any orientation to the earth. Some are polar, while others circle the earth from other angles. Some have orbits synchronous with that of earth and thus remain over one fixed point. These are called geosynchronous orbits and are possible around 23,000 nautical miles high. In order to go into orbit, however, the satellite must be boosted to the proper altitude and velocity. The flight must reach a velocity of between 17,500–24,600 miles per hour to attain orbit. Velocities greater than 24,600mph allow a flight to escape the earth's gravitational pull.

Large rockets, mostly modified ICBMs, are used as space boosters with the satellite replacing the ICBM warhead as the payload. Standard American boosters are the Atlas and Titan, both developed from early ICBMs. The Atlas was used in the Mercury manned space flight program in the early 1960s and is still used to orbit a wide range of communications and navigation satellites. The real workhorse of the American space program is the Titan III booster, which has been designed to handle payloads varying in size for orbits of different heights. This flexibility is achieved by adding large solid-propellant rocket motors in several arrangements. In its most powerful configuration, the Titan III can lift 15 tons into an orbit 100 nautical miles high. The Soviets also use ICBMs as space boosters. Indeed the SS-6 ICBM, first flown in 1957 as the initial Soviet attempt at fielding such a missile, was a failure as a strategic weapon, but became the workhorse Vostok space booster and is still in use.

So many satellites are launched (the Soviets alone put up around 90 per year), that the large expense involved in one-time-use boosters became a strong argument for the development of multi-mission space shuttles. Even after its first flight, however, the United States space shuttle clearly will not be able to cope with the varied timing of satellite launches. It is generally believed that expendable boosters will remain in use and that the new American MX ICBM is destined to become an important member of the space booster stable.

Military satellites fall into four categories: surveillance, early warning, communications and navigation. There are also meteorological craft. Surveillance or reconnaissance satellites are either imagers or listeners. Imaging satellites to date have used high-resolution cameras able to distinguish objects one-foot long from an altitude of 100 miles or more. In low orbits of roughly 80 miles perigee and 200 miles apogee, they perform either panoramic search missions or detailed local coverage in orbits lasting approximately 90 minutes. These satellites carry a number of film packets, which are periodically ejected in canisters for recovery. The newest such satellite, the American KH-11,

Left: a Vostok space booster lifts from its launching pad carrying Soyuz 37 in 1980.

transmits its images electronically in near real time, but it is unique in this respect. Film-recovery satellites provide better resolution pictures, but near real time satellites have obvious benefits in timely reporting. The primary drawback of camera sensors, however, is that they have no capability at night or in bad weather. The next generation of imaging satellites coming in the mid-1980s may not use cameras as their main sensors, but rather side-looking airborne radar (SLAR) and infrared line scan which produces images nearly as good as TV pictures. Indeed, infrared sensors can see under camouflage and foliage and determine whether vehicle

Above: the complicated docking maneuver of the US space capsules Gemini 6 *and* Gemini 7 *took place on 15 December 1965.*

engines are hot or cold and their fuel tanks are full or empty. The US Air Force is developing an infrared sensor so sensitive that from a satellite platform it will be able to provide tactical surveillance of theater battlefields and precise characterization of ballistic-missile attacks.

Imaging satellites have had a profound effect on the military competition of the superpowers. With the Soviets bluntly rejecting the 'open skies' proposal of President Eisenhower and underlining their position by blowing Francis Gary Powers' U-2 photoreconnaissance plane out of the sky in 1960, attempts at strategic arms control had foundered throughout the 1950s. Indeed Valentin Zorin forcefully expressed the Soviet position in 1961 when he compared on-site inspection of military facilities to 'an international system of legalized espionage, which, of course, cannot be accepted by any state which is interested in its security and in the maintenance of world peace.' The U-2 flights had provided the United States with its first real look inside Soviet borders and provided the first hard information on the quantity and location of Soviet ICBMs. The result was the exposure of the 'missile

Left: the Gemini 6 *manned space capsule is launched by a Titan booster from Cape Kennedy (now Cape Canaveral).*

Right: this photograph of Gemini 7 *was taken from* Gemini 6 *during rendezvous and station-keeping maneuvers at an altitude of 160 miles.*

Below right: the Agena Target Docking Vehicle is approached by Gemini 8 *during the rendezvous phase of the mission.*

Bottom right: the USAF Manned Orbiting Laboratory and a modified Gemini capsule are shown in this artist's conception. The project was cancelled in the early 1960s.

gap' which had so enlivened the presidential campaign of 1960. In the aftermath of the U-2 incident, President Eisenhower was able to promise the Soviet Union that no more U-2s would fly over their territory, because the United States was about to launch the first photoreconnaissance satellite. Within two years, the Soviets were also launching such 'birds.'

Since that time, the superpowers have been able to keep increasingly meticulous track of each other's military developments. The development of photoreconnaissance satellites has been a boon to systematic military intelligence and has prevented repetition of the 'missile gap' type of pseudo-crisis in Soviet-American relations. They have also helped to prevent genuine crises, since each side can act on the basis of more-reliable information about the other. Satellite photography is largely responsible for the fact that the two superpowers have been able to negotiate two treaties and an agreement limiting strategic arms. The satellites with their omnipresent cameras make it possible for each side to ascertain that the other is not violating the agreement. The agreements expressly forbid interference with, or attempts to deceive, what are euphemistically termed 'national technical means.' Imaging satellites are so vital that the United States did not even acknowledge their existence officially until President Carter did so in 1978 as part of the debate on the SALT II Treaty. No military satellite pictures have ever been released to the public.

Another important type of intelligence-gathering satellite is the Sigint (signals intelligence) variety. Termed 'Ferret' satellites by the United States,

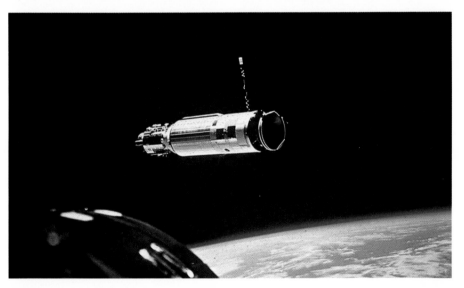

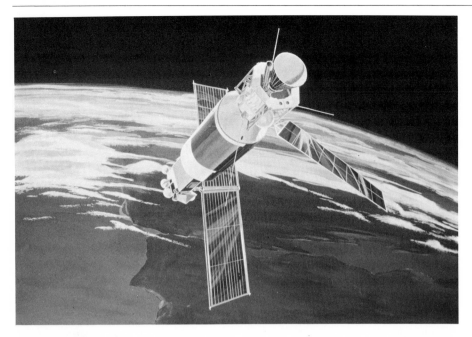

these devices intercept VHF, UHF and microwave transmissions. These electronic emissions are carefully analyzed by each side for information concerning military readiness, procedures and operations. The National Security Agency (NSA) was created by presidential directive in 1952 specifically to exploit communications intelligence and, subsequently, signals intelligence. Sigint rivals satellite photography in its importance to the military intelligence efforts of both sides.

A third variant of surveillance spacecraft are the early-warning satellites, which each side maintains in geosynchronous orbits over its opponent's ICBM fields. These vital craft rely on infrared sensors to detect the heat of ICBM exhausts 60 seconds after launch and thus provide the first warning of possible strategic attack. These satellites will report not just missile launches, but any strong infrared 'signature' and have on occasion raised the alarm by registering forest fires among other things. To minimize the possibility of misunderstandings, the SALT II Treaty requires each side to inform the other of pending ICBM test launches and not to launch more than one missile from a given complex at a time. The early-warning and reconnaissance satellites have become such an integral part of the strategic arsenals of the two superpowers that major interference with, or direct attack on, the satellites of the

other would be tantamount to a declaration of war, an obvious attempt to blind the enemy before attack.

Use of satellites for civilian and military communications has greatly expanded over the years. Some 70 percent of all United States military messages are now transmitted by satellite. The US Navy and Air Force are particularly active users of satellite communications. The Washington-Moscow 'hotline' has been routed through a series of American and Soviet comsats since the early 1970s. The most ambitious military comsat program is the US Defense Satellite Communications System Phase II, still under active development. Providing management, command, control,

intelligence and warning functions, the DSCS II uses voice, teletype, television, and digital-data modes to provide continuous communication between important military points and the US national command authority in Washington.

Each DSCS satellite weighs about 1350 pounds and measures about 38 feet from panel tip to panel tip, with a body 8.5 feet by 6.5 feet by 6.5 feet. The satellites are hardened, protected by antijamming features and have a service life of 10 years. The system is scheduled to comprise 15 satellites in geosynchronous orbits, but only four or so need to be active for the system to function efficiently.

The United States is totally dependent on these comsats in certain emergency situations. A DSCS I satellite played a key role in the rescue of the US ship *Mayaguez*, seized by the Cambodians in the early 1970s. President Nixon and his assistant Henry Kissinger were in real time communication with the rescue operations. The rescue team also received reports on the local weather via the satellite, thus eliminating the need for a weather aircraft which might have alerted the

Cambodians. DSCS II satellites were also key factors in planning the ill-fated Iran rescue mission in 1980. The next generation of military comsat, DSCS III, will begin to become operational in 1981.

Another ambitious satellite project underway is heralded as a revolutionary advance in warfare. The Navstar Global Positioning Satellite System is expected to solve two of the age-old problems in warfare, that of being uncertain of your exact location and that of your target or objective. Navstar, it is claimed, will enable a soldier to know exactly where he and his objective are located to within 30 feet. This capability should bring pinpoint accuracy to long-range ballistic missiles, make possible precision night bombing, and first-round kills in artillery fire. A lost soldier will have only to press a 'locate' button in a 20-pound radio pack and Navstar will send back his coordinates and further inform him of the compass heading for and distance to his objective. This will be possible because of 24 satellites scheduled to begin orbiting in 1981. In orbits of 10,900 miles, the Navstar satellites will carry super-high-speed computers and atomic clocks so accurate that they lose only one second in 30,000 years. Add scrambled communications for security to this supersophisticated hardware and Navstar emerges as far more than an ordinary exercise in triangulation. The United States ultimately expects to employ some 27,000 ground receivers for the Navstar system. 'The implications,' said one analyst, 'are so staggering that the strategic and tactical doctrine of our forces will have to be rewritten' if Navstar does solve the basic problem of location in warfare.

The militarization of space, which began over two decades ago with the first reconnaissance satellites, is now being pushed from passive surveillance, navigation and communications functions to active deployment of space-

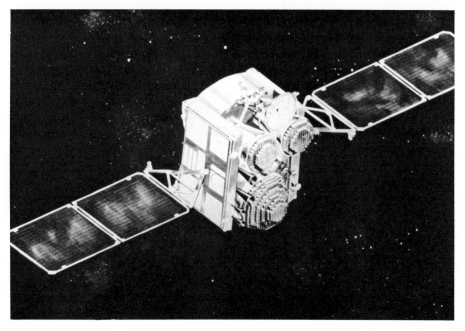

Right: the Defense Satellite Communications System, Phase III, will begin to replace earlier systems during 1981.

Left: Relay was a NASA communications satellite experiment, which was launched by a Thor Delta booster in December 1962.

Below left: technicians assemble a Skynet Comsat at Cape Canaveral in December 1973.

Right: an artist's conception of one of the Global Positioning System navigation satellites, 24 of which are to be placed in orbit.

Below: operators man their consoles at the satellite control center of the Defense Meteorological Satellite Programs, near Fairchild AFB, Washington.

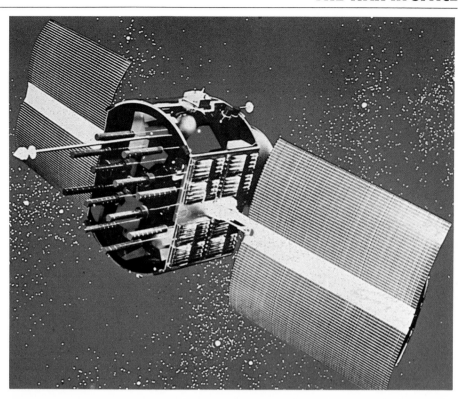

based weapons by the very importance and success of the passive missions. Although very cost effective in their missions, the passive satellites are very vulnerable and their real cost in the future may well be the cost of defending them.

Satellites can be attacked or degraded in a number of ways. Direct-ascent systems calculate the position of a satellite at a given time and launch an interceptor missile to explode a small nuclear warhead in that vicinity. Neither side has shown interest in such systems, although the Soviet Galosh antiballistic-missile system has been thought to have some direct ascent potential against satellites. Since at least the early 1970s, the Soviet Union has had an operational orbital interceptor, identified in the press as a 'hunter-killer' satellite. The interceptor is launched into orbit, maneuvers itself near the target and then explodes like a hand-grenade with a conventional charge. The system is believed to be moderately effective against low-altitude satellites in orbits of up to 300 miles. Over the

years the Soviet Union has tested this system at least 17 times.

The United States is developing a different sort of orbital interceptor. This is the Vought Corporation's Miniature Homing Vehicle (MHV), a cylinder 13 inches long and 12 inches in diameter weighing 34 pounds. An F-15 fighter flying at high altitude literally whips the MHV into orbit at a speed of 17,500mph. Arriving in the general vicinity of its target, its sensors home in on the infrared radiation emitted by the target. With a small on-board computer directing its maneuvers, which are powered by dozens of minirockets mounted around its periphery, the MHV collides with its target. The target is destroyed not by explosives, but by the mass and velocity of the MHV which shatters anything it touches. The prime requirement for this system is a tracking capability which can determine the position and path of the target precisely enough.

Laser battle stations in space, which many observers feel that the United States could have in operation by the

early 1990s, could be used either to attack or defend satellites, as could the space shuttle which is potentially the most effective satellite destroyer of all. Satellites as complete systems – space vehicles, ground facilities, communications links – are vulnerable in all respects. The ground facilities can be sabotaged or attacked by airborne troops, aircraft or ballistic and cruise missiles. The up and down communications links can be jammed, or manipulated to carry false information. Satellites are also vulnerable to nuclear and nonnuclear electromagnetic pulse.

Satellite survivability has become an important military requirement. The communications links have to be protected and the satellites themselves hardened and equipped with devices to protect against laser or orbital attack. Against lasers, for example, devices which sense laser light can be attached to the satellites to trigger

Below: the US space shuttle was first tested in April 1981. The illustration shows the rocket boosters being jettisoned.

maneuvering rockets and deploy decoys to confuse radars. Maneuvering and decoys could also be effective against orbital or direct-ascent interceptors. Antijamming techniques are being improved and systems like DSCS II and Navstar are purposely designed to have a number of on-orbit spares. Up and down links increasingly are using higher radio frequencies (EHF or extrahigh frequency and SHF or superhigh frequency), which are harder to jam and less affected by nuclear effects. The survivability of ground stations is being improved by moving these facilities to the United States and Canada and the development of mobile ground stations to increase redundancy. The Soviet Union has no ground facilities outside its own borders, and those within are vulnerable to air and missile attack.

The problem is that defending satellites in these ways makes the systems themselves much more costly and reduces their efficiency. Satellite size has always been constrained by the relatively light weights which boosters can place in orbit. Defensive measures,

such as hardening, laser sensing devices and maneuvering rockets and their fuel, add considerably to weight at the expense of the satellite's mission.

The comparatively small satellites and space vehicles of the 1960s and 1970s will begin to give way to larger and more ambitious spacecraft and structures in the 1980s. This will occur because dependence on space boosters will be relieved by the advent of the United States space shuttle. It is scheduled to become operational in 1983 and could be followed by a Soviet version within a few years. The shuttle project has been the main thrust of the American space program for almost a decade. The Soviet Union has maintained a consistent emphasis over the years on manned space flight in their program and their shuttle is known to be a priority as well. Space shuttles will make possible a whole new era in space operations by providing quicker and easier access to space.

The idea of a reusable spacecraft has existed since the 1950s, but problems of inefficient propulsion and lack of know-

ledge of reentry heating and hypersonic dynamics (velocities many times greater than the speed of sound) made such a craft unfeasible. This early work in the United States was called the Dyna-Soar Orbital Glider program. The Soviets apparently referred to their early effort simply as *Kosmolyot* (spacecraft). The Dyna-Soar program was cancelled in 1963, but the vicissitudes of the Soviet program have not appeared in open sources. The highly successful manned space programs which both sides conducted in the 1960s and 1970s remedied the technological shortcomings to the point when the United States again began exploratory work on a shuttle in 1969. The formal design and development program began in 1972.

The American shuttle is officially designated the OV-102 Columbia Orbiter Vehicle and was finally launched on 12 April 1981. Three improved versions are now being built. The craft

Below: the space shuttle deploys the Inertial Upper Stage with its payload, which is used for deep space transport.

is roughly the size of a DC-9 aircraft and, unlike every other spacecraft was launched without previous unmanned test flights in space. The shuttle consists of four main elements: the reusable orbiter vehicle, three 375,000-pound thrust engines, the huge external fuel tank carrying over 500,000 gallons of liquid hydrogen and liquid oxygen and two reusable solid-fuel rocket boosters, which together contribute 2,900,000 pounds of thrust to lifting the 2250–ton package of shuttle, tank and two boosters off the ground.

On lift-off from either Kennedy Space Center in Florida or Vandenberg Air Force Base in California, the three engines of the shuttle, each drawing fuel from the external tank at a rate of 1220 pounds per second, and two boosters raise the package to about 28 miles altitude. The boosters are then jettisoned, decelerated by parachutes and recovered from the ocean for re-use. As desired orbital height and velocity are reached, the main engines are shut down and the external tank detached to fall into an ocean. It is the only expendable element of the shuttle. The orbital-maneuvering-system engines then fire to provide the remaining thrust needed to go into orbit. Overall, 12–15 minutes will be required for the shuttle to arrive in stable orbit.

Carrying a crew of from three to seven, the shuttle can remain in orbit between seven and 30 days. When its mission is completed, the orbital-maneuvering-system engines are used to get the shuttle out of orbit and back into the atmosphere for an unpowered, 30-minute aerodynamic descent and landing like an aircraft. During launch and reentry the 3G load will be less than that of a good roller coaster ride. In its passage through the atmosphere during landing, the nose cap and leading edges of the wings reach temperatures of over 2300 Fahrenheit. The shuttle is then refurbished for its next mission in a turnaround time originally designed to be two weeks, but which may in fact turn out to be as much as four months or more. Current planning calls

Left: for tests within the earth's atmosphere the space shuttle was carried by a modified Boeing 747 launch aircraft.

for 50 shuttle flights a year with each shuttle craft having a service life of 100 flights overall.

The 60-foot by 15-foot cargo hold of the shuttle can carry 65,000 pounds of assorted payloads. One such payload will be unmanned interplanetary probes, which the shuttle will start on their journey from 600 miles altitude, thus sparing them the stress of booster launch. Another important payload will be the space laboratory being developed by the European Space Agency. The shuttle will be a boon to the satellite business, because it can deploy, service, repair, refuel or retrieve these spacecraft. Indeed the process will have similarities to the sleek, satellite-swallowing spacecraft in the James Bond film *You Only Live Twice*. In wartime the shuttle could also be used for manned command and control functions and strategic reconnaissance.

The mission with the most import is the lifting of the heavier satellites of the coming generation into orbit and the ferrying of component parts into orbit to be assembled into space stations, laboratories and perhaps ultimately factories. Both the United States and the Soviet Union have already orbited small manned space laboratories. The American laboratory came down in a

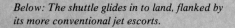

Below: The shuttle glides in to land, flanked by its more conventional jet escorts.

Above: the space shuttle places a satellite in orbit. The shuttle will enable larger and heavier payloads to be positioned in space.

fiery deorbit after its orbit decayed beyond repair, while the Soviet Union has worked hard to keep its lab up. While the shuttle may be the first step in the industrialization of space, its short-term effect will be to make possible the deployment of larger, more sophisticated, defended satellites, 'battlestar' laser or particle-beam space platforms for antisatellite and anti-ballistic missile use, and large space stations. The battlestar concept is a network of satellites to defend the passive satellites. In military terms, the shuttle will usher in a transition from passive to more active uses of space, such as missile and satellite defense, manned reconnaissance and command and control.

The main limitation of the current shuttle model is that it is confined to altitudes of 600 miles and below, yet many payloads, especially geosyn-chronous satellites, require far higher orbits. To meet this need, the Air Force is developing what is called the 'inertial upper stage' (IUS). This craft will be deployed by the shuttle to carry pay-loads to orbits as high as necessary. Also in development is a small space-ship, which the shuttle will deploy and leave in orbit to be collected again by later shuttle missions when the smaller craft has completed its own missions.

These developments will not occur without some major organizational and management changes in the United States space program. The shuttle has been a NASA project to date and NASA tends to see the shuttle as an end in itself. The shuttle's major customers, however, are the armed forces, which plan to launch shuttles from a special facility at Vandenberg Air Force base. In addition to its uses as a civilian space vehicle, from the beginning the shuttle has been intended to become the spacegoing arm of the armed forces. The conflict between civilian and military interests is probably inevitable and revolves to no little extent around the scheduling of shuttle flights. One response by the Air Force has been to question plans to phase out expendable boosters, so as not to lose the ability to meet priority national security needs in light of the technological and managerial uncertainties of the shuttle program at this stage.

In the military competition in space, the United States early took and still maintains the lead in unmanned space exploration, as the spectacular Voyager flights to Saturn and Jupiter in 1980 underlined. Excepting the shuttle the US has not had a man in space since 1975, when three astronauts linked up with two Soviet cosmonauts in the famous 'handshake in space.' The Soviet Union in the meantime has flown numerous manned missions, one lasting 185 days which set a new space-endurance record. The Soviet *Salyut 6* space laboratory has been in orbit since 1977 and the Soviet Union has said that it plans to develop Salyut into a 'per-manent orbital space station with inter-changeable crews.' The Soviets have been working toward this goal since 1969 when their *Soyuz 4* and *Soyuz 5* spacecraft linked up to create what amounted to a four-man, temporary space station. Since that time, Soviet manned space operations have consistently focussed on 'the concepts of resupply and crew change – psychological more than technological break-throughs,' as they investigate various aspects of long-term exposure in space. The Soviet Union clearly sees great potential in space and it has been laying a firm human as well as technological foundation for realizing its ambitious manned space goals.

The Soviet Union announced in 1978 that it had developed a prototype, winged reusable manned spaceship. Soviet designers have been at work on a shuttle-type craft for at least as long as the Americans, if not longer. But in 1980 the Soviet Union upgraded the transport version of its Soyuz space-craft, the workhorse of its space program, to carry three people and announced plans to expand the Salyut station by docking additional craft to it. This suggests that the Soviet shuttle program may not be as advanced as previously thought and that the Soviets have had to postpone their plans for a large space station in favor of this interim measure.

The shuttle will radically alter the competition in space by restoring the United States' lead in manned flight. It will also give the United States a strong advantage in the development of large space structures such as battle-stars and the large solar-powered space stations connected to earth by laser or microwaves now in advanced conceptual stages. As long as the Soviet Union remains dependent on rocket boosters, it will be losing ground in key areas, especially in important military capabilities.

Overall, however, it is the passive uses of space – communications, reconnaissance, early warning, navigation and meteorology – that will remain most crucial in peace and war. It is not yet efficient to place large weapons in orbit while they can be used as effectively on earth. The one exception could be the antiballistic-missile and antisatellite missions because missile warheads are most vulnerable as they loft through space. Thus the blazing battlestars of the futurists could be only a decade or so away and could finally break the bondage in which the superpowers have been held for 20 years by their massive material, intellectual and emotional investment in their ICBM arsenals.

'What is the military situation after we have had this tremendous exchange?' was the question in the Armed Serivces Committee of the US House of Representatives in 1964. The reply was, 'We are all dead.' This simple statement about the potential of strategic bombardment in World War III reflects the central military fact of the second half of the twentieth century. Both the United States and the USSR possess the means to destroy each other (plus quite a few other unfortunates) without engaging in warfare as it has been heretofore known and without defeating the armed forces of the opponent. The vehicle of this awesome power is the intercontinental ballistic missile or ICBM, a marriage of the fusion bomb and the long-range ballistic missile. Both countries have poured vast amounts of money and resources into the development and continuing refinement of these arsenals, which have become the visible measure of their relative politico-military power and standing in the world. Other countries like Britain and France have strategic nuclear weapons that must be reckoned with in any future war and the People's Republic of China even has a handful of ICBMs, but none enjoy such benefits and suffer such anxieties as do the United States and USSR from their ICBM forces.

The history of rockets stretches back to the thirteenth century, but their military applications have not been very effective until recently. During the War of 1812, for example, the British employed rockets, but primarily for their presumed shock value (thereby inspiring Francis Scott Key to write of 'the rockets' red glare' in what later became the American National anthem). The rocket really did not begin to come into its own until the Germans in World War II developed the liquid-fuelled rocket and a basic guidance system. Dubbed by Hitler

Overleaf: Sprint and Spartan missiles of the US Army Air Defense Command. US ABM defenses were dismantled in 1976, but may be reinstated.

Right: long-range ballistic missiles require precision in manufacturing. A technician examines the nose cone of a Thor IRBM.

the V2 (*Vergeltungswaffe 2* or 're-taliation arm 2'), the German A4 rocket was in essence a small ICBM. Launched vertically with a 2000-pound warhead and a self-contained guidance system based on gyros and an accelerometer, the missile reached an apogee of 60 miles on its 200-mile journey. Over 10,000 were produced and some 1100 launched against England alone. The V2 was far from a decisive weapon, but by the war's end the German rocket scientists had developed more advanced second generation models as well as a two-stage version for bombardment of the United States. The United States and USSR were both heavily dependent on V2 technology (and their transplanted German scientists) for their early generations of rocket weapons.

The development of ICBMs and shorter range ballistic missiles has made possible the effective strategic bombardment of the enemy homeland, a feat never really accomplished in World War II until the atomic bombing of Japan. The goal of strategic bombing was to reduce the enemy ability to support the war and break civilian morale. Targets were thus the factories, transportation systems and energy complexes of the industrial sector and the civilian population in the cities. Postwar analysis found the bombing to have been fairly ineffective. This was partly because of limitations on deliverable payloads, partly because of poor target selection due to inadequate intelligence and erroneous judgment, but more because German industry demonstrated amazing recuperative powers and the civilian population bore up

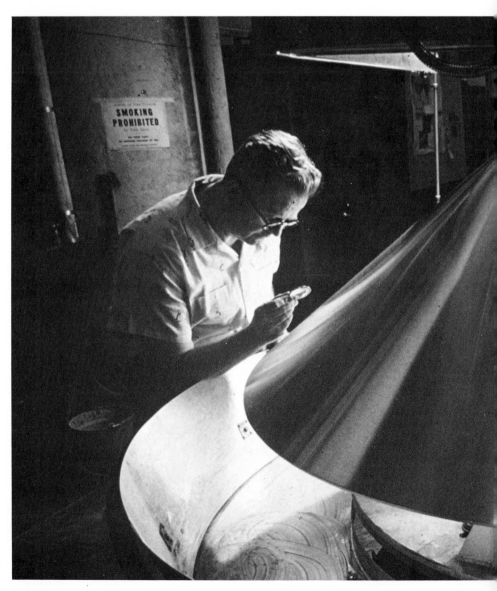

SMOKING PROHIBITED

well under the terror and hardship of repeated air attack.

Another important factor was accuracy, or the lack of accuracy. Precision bombing was found impractical despite prolonged attempts, especially by the US Air Force. Techniques of pattern bombing were developed as a result, but even so no more than 20 percent of the bombs dropped fell in their target areas, defined as a circle with a 1000-foot radius around the aim point. This problem was compounded by the difficulty of locating and hitting smaller industrial targets. The marvel of the ICBMs of the late 1970s and early 1980s is that they are expected to land in circles with considerably smaller radii drawn around targets whose coordinates and characteristics can be precisely determined.

Above: An Atlas missile lifts off at Patrick AFB, Florida on 24 August, 1959, on a test flight.

The development of rockets as weapons, particularly as strategic weapons, was rapid in the postwar period and was closely linked to the development of nuclear weapons. On 10 February 1954 the United States Strategic Missiles Evaluation Committee headed by John von Neumann reported the possibility of major technological breakthroughs in the size of nuclear warheads and the probable solutions to other problems related to large ballistic missiles within a few years. Within a month of this report, its predictions had been borne out in operational tests. The key factors were reducing the size and weight of the nuclear warhead, a trend which continues to this day, and developing a guidance system which would allow the warhead to be deposited somewhere in the vicinity of its target, another trend which continues to the present. Thus the two major advances in the early 1950s were the fusion bomb, which offered a far greater 'bang' than the fission bomb, and the ballistic missile, which was a far more efficient delivery system than the long-range bomber. The ballistic missile arrives on target in little more than 30 minutes after a 5000–6000 mile journey, most of which is spent in untouchable

Above: technicians prepare to remove a Titan I from its silo at Lowry Air Force Base during deactivation of the missile site in 1965.

inner space where it is virtually impossible to take effective countermeasures against it.

The early ICBMs were large and relatively unsophisticated. The Soviets flew the SS-6 (SS stands for surface-to-surface) in 1957, a missile so huge that it required 32 engines firing in concert to function. As one observer noted, this was '29 more than we are ever likely to see again.' It was a failure as a strategic weapon, only a handful of SS-6s were ever deployed, but the missile did find other important employment. One of its first jobs was launching *Sputnik I* into orbit. The first American ICBM was the Atlas, which was also a large missile despite having a launch weight some 40 percent less than the SS-6. With Convair as the prime contractor, it was rushed through a shortened development program. Its first launch was in June 1957 and its first operational launch by a Strategic Air Command (SAC) crew came in September 1959. The first Atlas complex was located at Vandenberg Air Force Base in California. The first version to be deployed in any number was the Atlas D with the

General Electric Mk 3 Ablative Reentry Vehicle.

Early deployment was in above ground, 'soft' sites and the only measure to reduce their vulnerability was geographic dispersal. Concern over the assumed Soviet threat during the 'missile gap' era led to a decision to place most of the force in silos (a reinforced concrete and steel structure designed to withstand overpressures of several thousand psi and to reduce thermal and radiation effects). The silo is intended to minimize the vulnerability inherent in soft sites. A soft site could be put out of action even by the dynamic pressure from a large warhead, let alone the overpressure, thermal and radiation effects. However, a one-megaton warhead would have to be detonated at ground level within 600–700 feet of the target to destroy a silo. Silos would have been a perfect means of ensuring the invulnerability of each side's ICBM

force, were it not for the near-simultaneous appearance of the photoreconnaissance satellite. For two decades the cameras of these spacecraft have mapped the precise coordinates of each and every missile silo and other important aim point. Prior to the advent of strategic photoreconnaissance, neither side could seriously consider attacking the opponent's embryonic ICBM force because locations were known only in the most general terms. It is only now that precise reconnaissance is finally being mated with precise missile accuracies to create a serious threat to the silo as a protective measure.

Concurrent with the development of the SS-6 and Atlas, the Soviet Union and United States were both at work on a second generation of ICBM, roughly comparable in technical characteristics. Both sides felt that prudence dictated development of additional ICBMs, because the technological un-

certainties of the whole endeavor were so great. The United States therefore produced the Titan I and II and the Soviet Union the SS-7 and SS-8 and put them into the field shortly after their first generation ICBMs.

The Titans profited from American experience with the Atlas and were designed to be silo based with inertial guidance, subsequently altered to radio guidance. Beginning development in 1955, the program was marked by many failures and did not reach operational status until 1962. Deployment was completed in early 1963 with two SAC squadrons at Lowry Air Force Base (Colorado) and one each at Beale (California), Mountain Home (Idaho), Ellsworth (South Dakota) and Larson (Washington) Air Force Bases. Each had nine missiles, making a total of 54. Titan I was obsolete even before it was deployed and was phased out in favor of Titan II. Virtually the only thing the missiles had in common besides their name was the same silo. Titan II had twice the range/payload capability of its predecessor, a new all-inertial guidance system which markedly improved flight performance, and a substantially improved reentry vehicle. This system became operational in 1963 with 54 missiles deployed in two squadrons each at Davis-Monthan (Arizona), Little Rock (Arkansas) and McConnell (Kansas) Air Force Bases. These missiles have been continuously operational since that time.

The Soviet second generation of ICBMs was almost as long-lived as the American missiles. Similar to the Titan, the SS-7 entered service in 1961 with what is believed to have been radio-inertial guidance, which later probably was altered to pure inertial guidance like the Titan II. Early deployment was in soft sites, but about 75 percent of the force was placed in impressively hardened silos. Around 190 SS-7s were put into the field. Only about 19 SS-8s were deployed, as this missile was apparently considerably less satisfactory than its sibling. As part of the SALT I Interim Agreement on Strategic Offensive

Left: the first Titan II launch took place at Vandenberg AFB in 1965. Note the missile exhaust venting from the silo.

Forces signed by the United States and USSR in May 1972, the SS-7 and SS-8 and the Titan II were classed as 'older ICBMs.' These could not be replaced with newer missiles, but they could be deactivated and replaced with ballistic-missile-carrying submarines at a prescribed ratio. The Soviet Union exercised this option and had deactivated the entire SS-7 and SS-8 force by 1977, but the United States has maintained the Titans as an operational part of its strategic forces at the price of three additional missile submarines. This is apparently a legacy of a verbal agreement between President Brezhnev and President Nixon at the signing of SALT I that the United States would not exercise this option.

The early ICBMs were unreliable and downright dangerous, using liquid fuels of highly corrosive and volatile chemicals. The Titan, somewhat better in this respect than the rest, uses nitrogen tetroxide as its oxidizer and hydrazine and unsymmetrical dimethylhydrazine as fuel. The oxidizer and the fuel ignite on contact. At least half a dozen US Atlas and Titan ICBMs have exploded in their silos in addition to many mechanical failures. The Titan force now stands at 52 because two missiles have been destroyed in their silos. The most recent incident occurred on 19 September 1980 when an eight-pound wrench socket accidentally fell 70 feet down the silo during maintenance and ripped a hole in the skin of the missile, which exploded killing two workers. Over 125 lesser incidents are reported to have occurred in the previous five years.

Prior to Titan II, missiles did not use storable propellants, but had to be fuelled as part of the launch procedures. This meant they had very slow reaction times. The Titan II by contrast can keep its fuel and oxidizer aboard for

Below: comparative views of Soviet and United States intercontinental ballistic missiles, including fifth generation ICBMs.

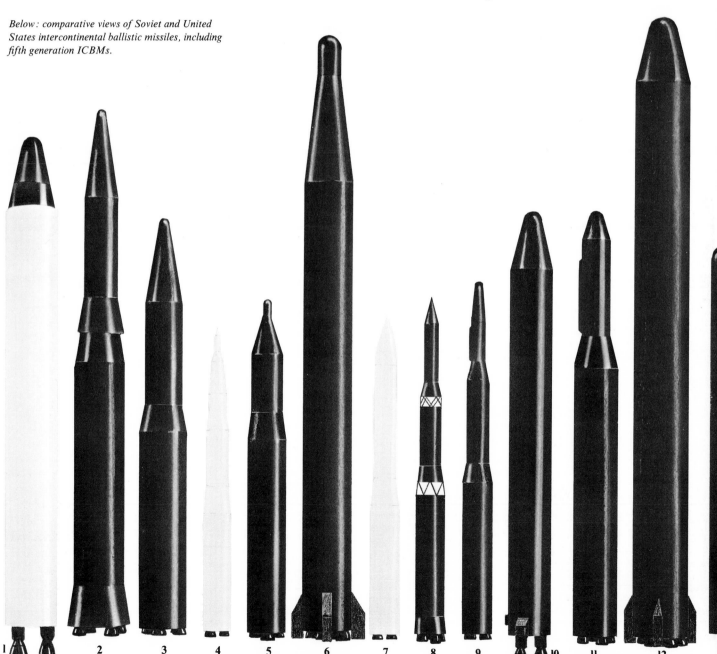

14　　15　　16　　17

months without boiloff, evaporation or undue corrosion and thus has a reaction time of close to a minute. Titan II was also the first missile able to be fired from inside its silo. The other ICBMs had to be hoisted to the surface, fuelled and then launched.

The Atlas had so many problems that it was phased out in 1965, rather than as planned in 1969. The Titan was originally scheduled for retirement in 1971, but Henry Kissinger, then National Security Advisor to President Nixon, had them kept in service in an unsuccessful effort to trade their retirement for a reduction in the size of the Soviet SS-9 heavy ICBM force. With their nine-megaton warheads, the Titans account for about one-third of aggregate United States megatonnage and thus keep the strategic balance from looking too lop-sided. They are too inaccurate to have any other mission than blasting Soviet cities, which is not currently part of declared United States' doctrine. Domestic politics since 1972, however, have made it unwise for any American administration to attempt to dismantle the Titan II force without exacting some concession from the Soviet Union. Thus, as former Secretary of Defense Melvin Laird has said, the Titans have 'just stood around without having a meaningful mission.'

The technological characteristics of the early ICBMs and the experience with strategic bombardment in World War II dictated their employment strategy. Their invulnerability in silos, their very large warheads, their very poor accuracies and their slow reaction times combined to rule out finely tuned employment options and made them bludgeons of general threat and weapons of last resort. Warhead size ranged from the four megaton of the Atlas and Titan I up to nine and 10 megatons of the Titan II and the Soviet missiles. Accuracies ranged from the 1500 meters of the Titan II to about 1800 meters for the other United States missiles and an estimated 2500 meters for the Soviet missiles. The only mission these missiles could really be expected to perform was city busting.

The United States thus adopted a doctrine called massive retaliation in the 1950s. As it lacked the military cap-

ability to protect its allies and clients all around the vast perimeter of the USSR, the United States reasoned that Soviet aggression could be deterred by the threat of a devastating nuclear attack on the Soviet periphery. Proponents of this theory, most notably Secretary of State John Foster Dulles, believed that such an attack would never occur because the threat alone would restrain the Soviet Union. Lacking strategic delivery means of their own, the Soviets, even after they developed nuclear weapons, could do nothing but hold Western Europe hostage in turn to their powerful theater forces. And so the military counterbalance of United States strategic power against Soviet land power was effected in the 1950s.

The equation could only be maintained, however, as long as the Soviets believed that the United States nuclear advantage could and would be employed. Once the Soviets acquired even a few ICBMs, massive retaliation became less and less appropriate. For the first time, an enemy had the means to breach the historic impregnability of the United States behind its two ocean barriers. The United States could no longer serve, as it had in World War II, as the sanctuary, granary and arsenal of its allies. As I Zavilov put it in the Soviet armed forces newspaper *Red Star* in 1970, 'The advent of nuclear rocket weapons provides a material basis for the principle of simultaneous striking of the enemy throughout the whole depth of his battle and operational formations, and the destruction of the most important military-economic targets in the deep rear of the combatant states.' Even from the mid-1950s massive retaliation had had critics, like the British military theorist Sir Basil Liddell Hart and the American Henry Kissinger. They argued that a defense based solely on massive retaliation was dangerous because limited war and specific military contingencies were still possible, as Korea had demonstrated in the early 1950s. The problem with massive retaliation and the ICBMs which became its blunt instruments in the late 1950s was that it provided no intermediate levels of action or option between atomic war at one end of the spectrum and appeasement at the other.

Top: an aerial view of a Minuteman launch site at Vandenberg Air Force Base, California. US ICBM test firings are carried out here.

Above: a cutaway drawing of a Minuteman III site, showing the missile in its silo and the launch-control facility.

not a result of coherent planning, but was simply the outcome of independent programs pursued by the Navy and Air Force, each of which wanted a 'piece of the action.' It was soon realized, however, that this diversity had the benefit not only of improved survivability of the strategic forces, but also severely complicated enemy strategic planning. Over the years interservice rivalry far more than strategic necessity has added the requirement that each leg of the triad be able to survive enemy attack independently of each other.

The United States triad is fairly well balanced between bombers and land- and sea-based missiles. The Soviet Union also has a triad of sorts but relies first and foremost on land-based missiles, only secondarily on sea-based missiles and very little on land-based bombers. The ground forces have historically been the most important of the services, but they were displaced to number two status in 1960 with the formation of the Strategic Rocket Forces (SRF) as a completely new service. The commander in chief of the SRF takes precedence over the other service chiefs without regard to actual rank. The SRF controls all land-based missiles with a range of over 1000 kilo-

Below: the nose cone of a Minuteman ICBM is mated to its booster in a silo at Vandenberg, AFB, California.

Massive retaliation had been a relatively cheap way for the United States to cope with its defense policy in the 1950s, but as the Kennedy administration took office in 1961, military policy was already being revised. President Kennedy and MacNamara continued and expanded this process to create a military and strategic doctrine that is still largely applied today. It was also during the early and mid-1960s that

both the United States and USSR began to field a third generation of ICBMs with much improved capabilities, as well as flotillas of ballistic-missile launching submarines. The United States also possessed a large force of strategic bombers, mainly comprising the new and powerful B-52. American strategic doctrine thus came to be based on a 'triad' of ICBMs, missile submarines and bombers. This was

94

meters. From its extremely modest original arsenal, the SRF has over the years come to possess the world's largest and most powerful missile force. It is on the basis of this force that the USSR has achieved a position of strategic equality with the United States.

Faced with the emerging strategic forces of the USSR and the defects of massive retaliation as the core of United States defense policy, MacNamara set out to reform both policy and forces. He rebuilt the moribund conventional forces of the United States and propounded the doctrine that the United States should have the capability to fight two major and one minor war simultaneously. His efforts in this area made it possible for President Johnson to place large forces in Vietnam in the mid-1960s without a prior period of mobilization and preparation. At the strategic level, Mac-Namara developed the Single Integrated Operations Plan (SIOP), which embodied a more finely tuned attack and discriminate targeting with some forces held in reserve. MacNamara underlined the move away from massive retaliation in his famous 'no cities' speech in 1962: 'The United States has come to the conclusion that, to the extent feasible, basic military strategy in a possible general war should be approached in much the same way that more conventional military operations have been regarded in the past. That is to say, principal military objectives, in the event of a nuclear war stemming from a major attack on the Alliance, should be the destruction of the enemy's military forces, not of his civilian population.'

MacNamara was searching for a way to make nuclear war fightable and still keep the nuclear exchange (for there now clearly would be an exchange) within tolerable limits. MacNamara explored a range of possibilities to keep such a conflict from degenerating into a mindless holocaust, including civil defense, ballistic-missile defense and the city avoidance/military-oriented targeting of his 1962 speech. However ballistic-missile defense was not technically feasible at that time and civil defense was met with public indifference.

Targeting military objectives is known as 'counterforce' and targeting cities and industrial objectives as 'countervalue.' MacNamara's doctrine of counterforce also had a number of problems. It clearly favored the United States with its superior strategic arsenal and was clearly provocative, because it could be construed as an American desire to attack the Soviet ICBM force rather than maintain a passive deterrent and retaliatory posture. It was never made clear whether MacNamara's doctrine required the United States to attack the USSR with its strategic forces in the event of a Soviet conventional attack on Western Europe.

Nor did counterforce seem likely to limit damage to the civilian sector. As James Wadsworth wrote in 1962, 'Because many cities are close to missile bases and airfields, it has been estimated that some 30,000,000 Americans would be killed in a first counterforce-type attack. The first bombs to fall would knock out most communications and reconnaissance facilities. Neither government could know whether the other side was "playing the game," which forces were still in existence, and what its own men were doing. In such confusion, total war would be almost inescapable.' Damage limitation also required the cooperation of the other side, but the Soviet Union refused to co-

Right: loading a Minuteman ICBM into its silo is a delicate operation. This missile was pictured at Edwards AFB, California.

operate. Commenting on the possible Soviet response to a limited American counterforce attack, a leading Soviet commentator on strategic affairs stated 'There are as yet no rules of behavior in a nuclear war.'

From the early 1960s to the late 1970s, the ICBMs of each side were seen as invulnerable to a surprise counterforce attack because neither side possessed the technical capabilities to carry out such an attack. There was in essence a strategic military stalemate which was termed mutual deterrence, the successor to massive retaliation. The invulnerability of the respective ICBM forces meant that either side was assured of the strategic capability to inflict unacceptable damage on the other in the event of a surprise attack. In these circumstances, so the theory went, no rational leadership could seriously opt for initiating a nuclear war. As the Soviet Minister of Defense Marshal Grechko wrote in 1971, the decision for nuclear war 'could only be made by an idiot or a man who has lost his mind.' The 'mutual' in this concept of deterrence was underlined by a statement of the Central Committee of the Soviet Communist Party, 'The atomic bomb does not adhere to the class principle; it destroys everybody within range of its destructive action.'

While tacitly agreeing that no rational leadership would launch a nuclear war, both sides worried that war could come by accident, or that a local confrontation could get out of hand. Apart from the recurring confrontations over Berlin in the late 1950s and early 1960s, the most sobering episode for both sides was the Cuban missile crisis of 1962. With the United States 'quarantining' Cuba over the presence of Soviet medium- and intermediate-range missiles discovered on the island, the chances for an ultimate confrontation were high. 'The greatest danger,' said MacNamara, 'was not that Khrushchev would deliberately launch nuclear war, but that the situation might have gotten out of control,' while Khrushchev himself wrote in his memoirs that 'Of course I was scared. It would have been insane not to have been scared.' In the aftermath of the crisis, both powers did accept their

common interest in drawing some limits around nuclear weapons, an acceptance that has led to a number of modest agreements and treaties over the years.

After the Cuban missile crisis, the ICBM forces of each country began a period of rapid expansion and major technological improvement. The United States began to deploy its first ICBM of the third generation, the Minuteman, in 1963 and arbitrarily halted deployment in 1968 when force size had reached 1000 launchers. In 1966 the USSR began to deploy its third generation – the SS-9, SS-11 and SS-13 – and had reached a force size of over 1600 launchers when deployment was frozen by the Interim Agreement of SALT I in 1972. Except for the retirement of the 209 SS-7s and SS-8s, force size has remained static on each side. Both have instead refined their missiles in terms of technological performance to the point where employment options that MacNamara's strategists could only speculate about are now conceivable. The advances in capabilities of ICBMs are thus once again calling into question basic tenets of strategic doctrine.

The US third generation ICBMs, the Minuteman series, differed radically from the large liquid-fuelled ICBMs of the second generation. They are smaller, simpler, much more accurate, have much more rapid reaction times and burn solid rather than liquid fuel. The decision to develop a solid-fuel missile was inspired by the US Navy, which in 1955 began work on a solid-propellant submarine-launched missile. The advantages of solid fuel are that the missile can be kept on alert indefinitely, it is notably cheaper, needs perhaps 90 percent less crew, and has virtually instantaneous reaction time. Minuteman III, for example, has a reaction time of only 30 seconds and is the outstanding example of pushbutton intercontinental warfare. Warhead size was also reduced, better reentry vehicles (RVs) designed, and improved propulsion and airframe technology brought in. The missile had a swift engineering development and flight-testing

Right: six unarmed Minuteman III Mark 12 reentry vehicles streak across the sky near Kwajalein Atoll in the Pacific.

program in 1958–60.

The Minuteman is a versatile missile. It can be fired out of a simple hole in the ground and its silo requires no special venting of exhaust gasses, but it does give off an unusual smoke ring which is typical of Minuteman launches. One early option was to base the system in trains to create a mobile missile whose movement would make it even more secure than silo basing. The plan envisioned five squadrons on 10 trains with the missiles to be elevated and fired through split roofs. In 1979 a Minuteman was launched from its

96

canister off the back of a jeep just to prove that it could be done.

Minuteman deployment has differed from that of the earlier ICBMs in that large squadrons have been formed of silos dispersed over vast areas. Minuteman sites are unmanned and at least three miles from each other. Ten silos and a launch-control center manned by only two officers constitute a flight, and five flights a missile squadron. Three to four squadrons constitute a wing, of which there are six deployed at six locations in the midwest. The 50 silos and five launch-control centers of a squadron are all interconnected by a buried cable network, which enables each launch-control facility to monitor and launch all 50 missiles. It is also possible to launch the missiles from a SAC airborne command post. Two missile flights became operational at Malmstrom Air Force base (Montana) in December 1962. Within six months squadrons were operational at this base. An improved version with slightly longer range was deployed in 1963 and by mid-1965 the United States had an impressive force of 800 Minutemen.

In September 1964 a more advanced model began to be tested and some 450 were deployed. With the original version designated as Minuteman I, this new model became Minuteman II and 550 examples of a subsequent model, Minuteman III, were deployed. The Minuteman Is were retired and the United States ICBM force came to comprise 1000 Minuteman IIs and IIIs by 1968, marking the end of a very rapid evolution of force size and capability.

Minuteman I was a three-stage missile with a single ablative (meaning the skin burns away to dissipate heat during

reentry) RV. It reportedly carried a one-megaton warhead with an accuracy of 1000m and had a range of about 6000 miles. Minuteman II is a larger and heavier missile, which has a new guidance system giving greater accuracy and more target data-storage memory. The warhead is two-megatons and carries penetration aids or 'penaids' which usually means chaff and/or decoys to confuse enemy radars should any type of ballistic-missile defense be attempted. It was first deployed in 1966 at Grand Forks, North Dakota.

The most important changes, however, appeared with Minuteman III, the world's first MIRVed missile. Rather than one RV, the Minuteman III carried three 'multiple independently targeted reentry vehicles' or MIRVs. This revolution in missile technology suddenly tripled the number of warheads without increasing the number of missiles deployed. In a sense, the force became three times more efficient. The military significance of the introduction of the MIRV is that a MIRVed force need use only a fraction of its missiles to deliver a large number of warheads against the silos of the other side and still retain a large reserve of missiles. The innovation was controversial because it appeared to take the United States far beyond the needs of mutual deterrence, but it was argued that MIRVing the force was necessary to

Below: a Soviet intercontinental ballistic missile pictured in its silo.

penetrate the antiballistic-missile defense the Soviet Union was then deploying. Probably equally important was the fact that the technology was available to give the United States a cheap (albeit temporary) military advantage over the USSR. The original Mk 12 warhead had a yield of 170 kilotons and an accuracy of around 350m. The force is now being retrofitted with the Mk 12A warhead with a 350-kiloton yield and 225m accuracy. The Minuteman III silos have also been upgraded to improve their survivability and command and control features have also been improved.

The United States thus developed a force of small, reliable, relatively accurate missiles as its side of the strategic equation. The USSR took a different route and ended up with a more diverse but still highly effective force. The mainstay of the Soviet ICBM force until recently has been the SS-11, similar to the Minuteman but a little larger and still liquid-fuelled. The SS-11 has three versions, the original mod 1 (model 1) and the later mods 2 and 3. The mods 1 and 2 are single RV versions, while the mod 3 has three smaller RVs which are not independently targetable. The mods 1 and 2 are believed to carry a two-megaton warhead and have accuracies of 900m, while the mod 3 carries three 300-kiloton RVs, but its accuracy has not been published. The Soviets put over 1000 SS-11s into the field between 1966–72 in an impressive effort which balanced the United States Minuteman program.

Particularly disturbing to the United States was the fact that in addition to the SS-11s, the Soviets also deployed 288 SS-9s. These giant missiles carry in various versions warheads of 18–25 megatons, as well as a multiple-warhead version with three four to five-megaton warheads. Although accuracy was only believed to have been around 1300m, these weapons were interpreted in the United States as being a Soviet attempt to develop a 'hard target' capability because of their huge warheads. It was assumed that the mission of the SS-9 was to attack hardened command and control centers and missile silos, thus the United States went to great lengths to negotiate a limit of 308 launchers on

heavy missiles of this sort in SALT I.

The SS-9 was also a liquid-fuelled missile, but the Soviet Union did introduce the solid-fuel SS-13 missile. Only 60 launchers were deployed, and they remain operational to the present, even though the SS-13 is thought to be less capable than the workhorse SS-11. The Soviet Union has continued to design solid-fuelled missiles, the most successful to date being the SS-20 intermediate-range missile, but it still relies primarily on liquid-fuelled vehicles.

The rapid growth of this formidable force of almost 1600 ICBMs persuaded MacNamara that the missile race should be at least slowed, if not halted. In 1967 the United States made overtures to the USSR concerning negotiations on strategic-arms limitations, but the early contacts came to nothing after the Soviet invasion of Czechoslovakia in 1968. Formal talks began in 1969 and culminated first in the Interim Agreement of Strategic Offensive Arms in 1972 and subsequently in the Vladivostok Accords of 1974. The initiation of these talks was a formal United States recognition of the USSR as a strategic equal. It was also an admission that the USSR had effected one of the great shifts in the international balance of power in history. Based on the principle of overall equality, the negotiations were extremely difficult because of the problem of comparing two arsenals so different in their characteristics. The early agreements essentially codified the sizes that both strategic arsenals had already reached, but did not prevent the introduction of new ICBMs or the refinement of existing weapons. Even as the ink was drying on the Interim Agreement in Moscow on 26 May 1972, the USSR was already flight testing a fourth generation of ICBMs and the United States had one in the design stage.

The 1970s were truly the Soviet decade in terms of strategic forces. As the United States made a few improvements to Minuteman III and deferred others for lack of funds, while regularly postponing its new ICBM, the Soviet Union overhauled its entire ICBM force. Four new Soviet ICBMs were tested and three were extensively de-

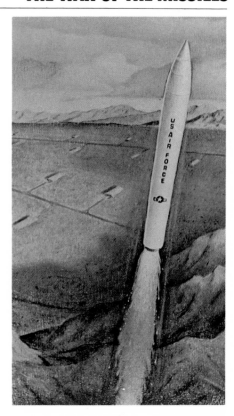

Above: an artist's conception of an MX missile launch. This fourth-generation ICBM is due to be deployed in 1986.

ployed. Between 1975–80 the Soviet Union replaced the entire SS-9 force with the SS-18 and replaced about half of the SS-11 force with the SS-17 and SS-19. The SS-18 is as big as the SS-9, but it has excellent accuracies of 550m in its mod 1 version and 350m in its mod 2. It can carry the big warheads of the SS-9, but it can also carry up to 10 MIRVs. Even with a SALT-permitted limit of 308 launchers, the SS-18 is fully capable of attacking American missile fields without assistance from the remainder of the Soviet ICBM force. The SS-19 with six MIRVs is equally accurate and the SS-17 with four MIRVs only slightly less so. The Soviet Union now has a formidable force of modern, accurate ICBM warheads, with an estimated 300 SS-19s and 150 SS-17s and the 60 SS-13 launchers in addition to what remains of the SS-11 force after modernization.

In the 1980s both sides will see yet another round of ICBM modernization. The Soviet Union is believed to have from two to four new ICBMs approaching the flight-test stage of development.

Under SALT II rules the Soviet Union would only be permitted to deploy one new ICBM system, but SALT II is almost certainly a dead letter in its present form and negotiation of a new agreement would take years. The Soviet Union thus has very good options for improving the quality of its force. Indeed the Soviet ability to design new, improved ICBMs dismays American officials. As former Secretary of Defense Harold Brown put it, 'We build, they build; we reduce, they build.' The demonstrable momentum of the Soviet strategic program was certainly the single most important factor in torpedoing the SALT II Treaty in the Senate in 1979 and in the triumph of demands for a tougher agreement.

Although the United States has had a fourth-generation ICBM, the Missile Experimental (MX), on the drawing boards since 1971, it is not scheduled for deployment until 1986 and will not reach its full force level until 1989. For domestic political reasons, the program has been postponed repeatedly. Although considerably smaller than the SS-18, the MX is designed to carry 10 MIRVs, the limit permitted in the SALT II Treaty. Both the SS-18 and the MX are believed to have the capability to carry more than 10 RVs if freed from the constraints of SALT. The MX, however, was conceived with the SALT environment in mind and the United States has found itself in a

dilemma as a result. The large growth in the number of Soviet warheads and their impressive improvements in accuracy mean that the American ICBM force is, at least theoretically, no longer invulnerable in its silos. The Soviet Union can target two or more RVs to each silo, which, coupled with the accuracy of fourth generation RVs, means a very high level of damage expectancy. There is a need to improve considerably the survivability of the United States' force, which can only be done through mobility and concealment. However, SALT requires that the number of missiles be verified by photoreconnaissance satellites, which is no problem with silos but almost impossible with mobile basing.

The MX itself is a three-stage solid-propellant missile weighing 95 tons, compared to the 39 tons of the Minuteman III. The missile will be super-accurate to within 100m, far surpassing anything the Soviet Union will conceivably have in the 1980s, because of its advanced inertial-guidance system. Its electronics and computer are 10 times as 'hard' as those of Minuteman III. It will be the world's most powerfull weapon and will give the United States what neither side has been able to acquire in two decades and more of ICBM research and development: a theoretical first-strike capability.

Yet it is entirely possible that MX, the creature of SALT, will never be

Right: the MX was not the first US conception of a mobile missile, as this artist's impression of a train-based Minuteman shows.

deployed because of SALT. The treaty requires that the Soviet Union be able to count the number of launchers and survivability requires that they do not know where the missiles are. As a result a number of extremely complicated and generally very expensive basing modes were devised in the late 1970s to answer the problem. One, the Multiple Aim Points System (MAPS), required the entire force of 200 MXs to be shuttled at random among 4000 silos or aim points, on the theory that the Soviets would have neither the warheads nor the operational capability to attack all 4000 silos. Such a plan was grossly at odds with the long-standing SALT ban on construction of new launchers. A second basing mode envisaged a system where the missiles, mounted on huge transporter-erector-launchers weighing 400 tons loaded, would again shuttle at random between a number of dispersed hardened shelters around an immense 'racetrack.' A series of such tracks in the western United States would contain a total of 4600 shelters to hide the missiles. Both the MAPS and racetrack systems would periodically open up to allow Soviet satellites to verify the number of missiles. Other basing suggestions have involved long, buried trenches with the missiles trundling along on tracks, dropping the missiles by parachute from aircraft, or deployment on small diesel submarines in United States coastal waters.

Some people questioned whether MX would ever, (or should ever), be built, because of its immense cost and dubious solutions to the dilemma. Yet most sober analysts in Washington in 1980 were betting that the missile would be built and deployed in Minuteman silos or new superhard silos, quite possibly defended by antiballistic-missile systems. Deployment of such defenses is banned by the Antiballistic Missile Treaty of 1972, but the treaty is re-

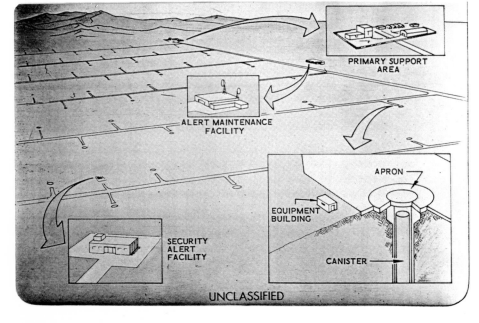

UNCLASSIFIED

PRIMARY SUPPORT AREA

ALERT MAINTENANCE FACILITY

EQUIPMENT BUILDING

APRON

CANISTER

SECURITY ALERT FACILITY

Left: an artist's concept of the MX missile vertical shelters. The basing mode of this missile has been the subject of much debate.

examined by each side at five year intervals. The whole issue of the vulnerability of ICBM silos, however, hinges first on the nature of ICBM accuracy and then on the operational capabilities of ICBM forces. It should be asked if ICBMs really are as accurate as they are represented and if it is really possible for either side to contemplate a first strike as a military operation, rather than a theoretical computer exercise.

The ICBM flies a trajectory of between 5000–6000 miles, during which it goes through specific stages. Missiles can be cold or hot launched. Cold launch means the missile is popped out of its silo by compressed gas and then its engines are ignited, thus sparing the silo a considerable amount of damage. The SS-19 and SS-18 utilize this technique and so will the MX. Hot launch means the missile engines fire in the silo, which requires a considerable amount of refurbishment afterward. Once out of its silo the missile has perhaps six to eight minutes of powered flight to get it up through the dense

Above right: the canister carrying the MX missile leaves its protective shelter and elevates to firing position.

Right: the most serious scheme for the mobile basing of MX is a series of 'racetracks' around which the missiles would be moved.

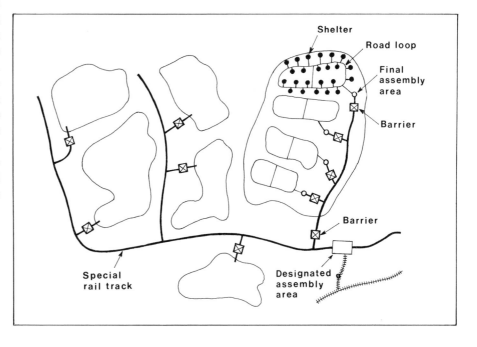

lower atmosphere to a height of some 60 miles and about the same distance downrange. At this point the engines shut down and the RV separates from the booster rocket in single warhead missiles. In MIRVed missiles, what is called the postboost vehicle (PBV) separates from the booster. The PBV is essentially a 'bus' which carries the RVs. The RV or PBV then lofts through space reaching an apogee of some 600 miles before falling back toward earth. By the time the atmosphere is reentered, the RV is travelling at around 12,000 mph. In this phase of the ballistic trajectory, the PBV must execute a complicated series of powered man-euvers to release one by one its cargo of RVs. This delicately timed sequence determines the accuracy of the MIRVs and it is in this last phase of the trajectory that the RVs are subject to strong and unpredictable aerodynamic forces.

Guidance for this long ballistic flight can come from radio command or inertial sensing. Radio was early tried by both countries, but it has the disadvantage of making the missile dependent on external links which can be jammed or otherwise fail. All third- and fourth-generation missiles use inertial sensing of one form or another. Guidance occurs only in the powered-flight phase. Inertial sensing uses gyro-scopes and accelerometers to measure the forces other than gravity influencing the motion of the missile. These instruments continuously monitor the location of the missile between launch and thrust termination. Very sensitive accelerometers measure the forces acting on the missile, while the onboard computer uses this information and a very accurate clock to compute the velocity and position of the missile. The computer directs the autopilot mechanism to steer and control the thrust until the actual velocity and the preprogrammed velocity coincide. The thrust must be terminated at exactly this point.

Numerous errors creep into the pro-

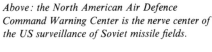

Above: the North American Air Defence Command Warning Center is the nerve center of the US surveillance of Soviet missile fields.

Left: the US Ballistic Missile Early Warning System unit at Thule, Greenland. Both sides rely heavily on such radars.

cess. The thrust is difficult to control and can result in target misses of up to 600m if turned off even one-thousandth of a second too late. The thrust of liquid-fuelled missiles is more amenable to finely tuned control than is that of solid-fuel missiles. Another source of error is the relative precision of the mathematical model of the earth's gravity which is used in computation. The guidance system must also be told with as much precision as possible the coordinates of the launch point and of the target, hence the sensitivity of geophysical measurements is an important factor. The gravitational effect of the sun and moon must also be included in the guidance equation. The engineering of the instruments themselves must be incredibly precise. A dust mote on an accelerometer can translate into several hundred meters of miss. Nor can either side test local anomalies of the earth's gravitational field over the North Pole, which is the flight path most ICBMs will take. The only test data comes from launches in other areas.

The United States launches its test missiles from Vandenberg Air Force Base, California to Kwajalein Lagoon in the Marshall Islands. The Soviet Union generally tests from several missile ranges in the western USSR eastward to the Kamchatka Peninsula. Both sides achieve consistently good accuracies in their testing, but the question of whether these accuracies will apply to polar trajectories does arise. Commenting on this fact in Congressional testimony in 1974, Secretary of Defense James Schlesinger said, 'It is impossible for either side to acquire the degree of accuracy that would give them a high confidence first strike, because we will not know what the actual accuracy would be like in a real world context.'

There is no such thing as absolute accuracy for ICBMs. The relative nature of accuracy is determined by the nature of the target and the desired damage effects. The main requirement is that the margin of error be less than the area of weapons effects that will cause the desired amount of damage to the target. The accuracy requirements for targeting hardened-point targets, such as missile silos and certain command and communications facilities, are quite different than those for airfields, industrial complexes, ports, or area targets such as troop concentrations. Against hard targets the yield of the weapon is no compensation for lack of accuracy, because the warhead must detonate in close proximity to the target. Modern hard targets, especially silos, can withstand considerable overpressures before their ability to function is impaired. The margin of error in counterforce targeting is quite small and thus the counterforce threat of ICBMs is directly dependent on their accuracy.

The relativity of ICBM accuracy is illustrated by the fact that it is measured in statistical probabilities. Missile RVs launched at a given target will fall in a distribution around the aim point. Accuracy is thus expressed as the radius of a circle around the aim point within which 50 percent of the RVs will land. Expressed in nautical miles or meters, this radius is called the Circular Error Probable (CEP). The other 50 percent of the RVs will fall within three CEPs of the aim point. If the CEP is one nautical mile, then half of the RVs will land within one nautical mile of the target and the rest within three nautical miles. Even with soft targets this is a significant miss for half of the attacking RVs and one reason why the older, less accurate missiles carried warheads with larger yields in modest compensation. If the CEP is 100 meters, as it is projected for the MX, even the warheads landing within three CEPs of the target will have accuracy better than many of the first generation ICBMs.

The actual CEP of a missile is determined during its flight testing. As adjustments and modifications are made to the missile the CEP improves. After a system has been operational for some years, it is referred to as having a 'mature CEP' as opposed to its initial CEP. Thus the CEPs of the SS-18 and SS-19 are currently thought to be around 315m, but they are expected to improve to around 220m by 1985. Replacing the Mk 12 with the Mk 12A RV on the Minuteman III will improve its CEP from 350–225m.

Accuracy is the dominant variable in calculating potential missile effectiveness, but a second important factor is reliability. Like accuracy, reliability is also expressed as a percentage of probability, in this case probability that the missile as a complex system composed of hundreds of subsystems

Below: an artist's conception of the Safeguard anti-ballistic missile system's area defense against attack by ICBMs.

will in fact work. Reliability is a percentage of the probability that the missile will ignite, lift out of its silo unscathed, roll to the proper orientation in azimuth, pitch over properly, not have a dust mote on its accelerometer and successfully release its RV or RVs.

All estimates of force vulnerability are dependent on characteristics such as accuracy, reliability, yield and silo hardness. In order to calculate damage expectancy or lethality, for example, these variables are used to calculate percentages of probability that the target will be destroyed, but these estimates are very sensitive to change in even one variable. For example if CEP changes from 220m to 440m, this alters the result by a good 50 percent. When strategic conflicts are modelled, as they are constantly in the United States and presumably also in the USSR, the models tend simply to multiply the effects of attack on one silo by the number of silos. This ignores the fact that ICBM forces (or any other forces for that matter) have operational aspects and are subordinated to a larger set of politico-military variables. Among these variables are the decisions made by the politicians on either side, the ability of the political leadership to communicate its decisions to its forces and the ability of the forces to execute the decisions.

Thus the simple measuring of one side's capabilities against those of the other in terms of quantitative measures and methodologies, as is common, is fraught with theoretical risks on one hand and practical dangers on the other. The theoretical risks are that quantitative strategic analysis is a seriously defective art, because the models are oversimple and cannot take account of all the operational factors which would really determine the outcome of a strategic nuclear exchange. The practical danger is that the results of such modelling may be taken as pragmatic guides to policy formulation. Indeed, one oft-demonstrated characteristic of the United States defense community is that contending parties use quantitative analysis to support their particular case. This has never been more evident than in the debate about the vulnerability of the ICBM force.

Apart from the theoretical estimates of force vulnerability, there are important operational factors which need to be considered. The most common scenario assumes that the Soviet Union launches a countersilo preemptive strike which leaves the United States with too few ICBMs for a counterattack on Soviet military targets. The only military response left to the United States is retaliatory attacks on Soviet cities with the bomber force and submarine-based missiles. However the Soviet Union still has a large number of ICBMs plus their large submarine-based missile force to attack American cities. The two options thus left to the United States president are the destruction of American cities or surrender. Such a scenario, however, completely ignores the staggering operational difficulties and uncertainties in executing a large, coordinated missile attack. Neither side can rehearse or even appear to be rehearsing measures to overcome the difficulties and reduce uncertainties. The United States keeps 80–90 percent of the Minuteman force on alert 24 hours a day. The Soviet Union reportedly maintains a much lower alert rate, perhaps as low as 25 percent, of its ICBM force and does not seem to fear a 'bolt from the blue' attack by the United States. Instead, it believes that, as indications of approaching conflict

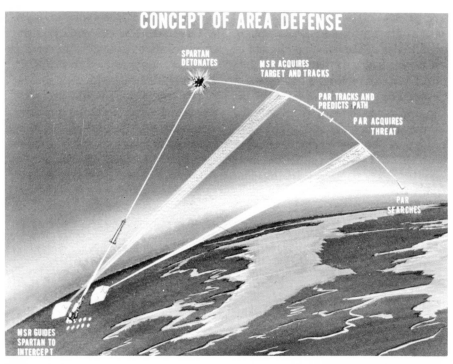

accumulate, it will have time to 'generate' its forces to an adequate level of readiness.

The initial problems that the USSR would face in contemplating a preemptive strike against United States silos would be preventing the United States from detecting the changing operational status of the Soviet ICBM force, and also that the United States force would already be largely generated. The next problem would be that the United States early-warning system would begin sounding the alarm within a moment or two of the Soviet launch. The United States would have about 30 minutes to verify that a real attack was underway, evacuate the president and other key political and military personnel and decide what its response would be. The two possible responses are to ride out the attack, or to launch on tactical warning (LOTW). The latter means launching some or all ICBMs when warning of the coming attack is received. The Soviet RVs would thus be attacking empty silos rather than reducing or eliminating the United States' ability to strike the USSR. The problem is that the warning may be a false alarm and there is no way to abort an ICBM attack once the missiles have been launched. False alarms recur, sometimes due to human error, but more often because of mechanical malfunction. The false alarm factor therefore makes LOTW politically risky for any United States administration to espouse as declared strategic doctrine. The Soviet Union, however, could never be certain what the United States response would be: LOTW, a retaliatory trading of United States for Soviet cities if the preemptive attack succeeded, or abject surrender. In the end the response would almost certainly be dictated by the personality and values of the American president, who alone holds absolute release authority over United States nuclear weapons. Apart from all the other operational uncertainties, how any individual would react to the choices presented by those crucial 30 minutes between launch and arrival on target can simply never be known until that unthinkable situation occurs.

A strong argument can in fact be made that the vulnerability of silos is the least of the strategic concerns of either side. As one analyst has noted, 'The command structure of modern strategic forces is much more vulnerable to attack than are the weapons themselves.' Positive command and control of strategic forces is probably the central problem in nuclear warfare. As one Congressional report said, 'Nothing ought to be of more concern . . . than the extraordinarily good ability to command, control and communicate with strategic forces before they are attacked and the very poor ability thereafter.' The vulnerability of its C^3 is probably the main limiting factor for each side in its strategic planning. Both sides, but especially the Soviet Union, have been paying more attention to this problem and trying to increase the survivability of their C^3 through hardening, redundancy and land and air mobility. Thus successful conduct of nuclear war, let alone a preemptive strike, requires a battle management

Below: the Spartan was the long-range interceptor of the Army's Safeguard Ballistic Missile Defense System, which was phased out in 1976.

Below left: the Sprint was the short-range, high-acceleration missile of the Safeguard System. It is pictured during a 1969 test.

Below: the Perimeter Acquisition Radar (PAR) was the long-range eye of the US Army's Safeguard ABM system.

Bottom: an aerial view of a Safeguard missile site. The Missile Site Radar is the pyramid-like structure, with the missile field foreground.

capability which either side would be foolish to think it possessed.

If a massive preemptive attack is not feasible as a military operation, how then would ICBMs be employed in wartime? This is a question which has only recently begun to receive serious consideration, because ICBMs will never be used in wartime if they are properly performing their deterrent function. Now that the improved technological capabilities of ICBMs are casting some doubt on the continued viability of mutual deterrence, the key problem for both sides is, as Christophe Bertram has written, that 'nobody knows what will happen once deterrence has failed. Both sides are willing to deter and to cope with considerable costs in this respect. But their doctrines, which have been developed for deterrence, will not be suitable for a situation that will come about once deterrence has collapsed. The United States and USSR have already accepted that nuclear war is possible and they are actively exploring the operational implications of this acceptance. The most likely scenario is now thought to be a period of growing political crisis, followed by conventional and perhaps theater nuclear combat in Europe and the Far East, and finally limited nuclear strikes on military targets in the United States and USSR. Both sides should thus have more than adequate time to have their strategic forces fully generated, to protect their governmental apparatus as much as possible and to prepare their civilian populations as far as they can. Strategic nuclear war will more than likely be reluctant, cautious, selectively limited, and probably conducted with the possibility of ending that aspect of the war through negotiation as soon as possible.

It seems likely that both sides will simply have to live with some element of vulnerability associated with their ICBM forces. This will be easier for the Soviet Union since it has had to accept strategic inferiority for almost three decades and harder for the United States, which still suffers from a 'Pearl Harbor syndrome' or morbid fear of surprise attack. There is a growing possibility that ICBMs will lose much of their stultifying grip on the politico-military relationship of the superpowers

Below: the Combat Operations Center of the North American Air Defense Command is located below the granite of Cheyenne Mountain, Co.

very effective even against third generation ICBMs.

The United States and USSR signed a treaty in 1972 which limited each side to 200 interceptor missiles, subsequently reduced to 100. The United States deployed a few interceptor missiles in defense of an ICBM site in the early 1970s, but deactivated these by 1976. The Soviet Union has deployed only 64 Galosh interceptors around Moscow.

The ABM treaty does permit research and development and, as Barry Smernoff has noted, 'Time and technology move on.' Developments in ABM technology have clearly outrun the ABM treaty and its premises. Both sides are believed to have the capability to produce effective laser ballistic-missile defenses, which could be either ground or space-based, by the early 1990s. There is more uncertainty about the feasibility of particle-beam weapons, but these remain a possibility. Meanwhile the Soviet Union is improving its ABM defenses around Moscow, as permitted by the treaty. The United States will begin testing a low-altitude system in the mid-1980s. This is essentially a much improved version of the Sprint, and will be used with a high-altitude system to provide a layered defense. United States prospects for future ABM developments are probably considerably better than those of the Soviet Union. The army, which is responsible for United States ballistic-missile defense, believes that it has the technology to build an effective terminal-defense system 'that can detect, discriminate, and intercept ICBM warheads, even in the extreme environment caused by massive ICBM attacks, ICBM (rocket booster) tank fragments and penetration aids.' The most likely mission of the coming generation of ABM systems is the point defense of MX sites and important C^3 facilities.

The full development of ABMs as operational weapons is, however, a factor that will not begin to come into play until the 1990s and later. Both sides have such a huge economic and politico-military investment in their ICBM arsenals that these rapid and powerful weapons will remain an important factor in any future major war regardless of other developments.

Above: Minuteman multiple independently targeted reentry vehicles are shown with the protective nose cone removed.

during the 1980s, because effective defenses could at last become possible.

Neither side has yet succeeded in mounting an effective defense against ballistic missiles. The immense technical difficulties involved have been likened to trying to stop one bullet with another. Indeed the difficulties have been so great that both sides have mutually foresworn more than token deployment and have relied on deter-rence rather than active defense. The development of antiballistic missile (ABM) programs began almost concurrently with that of the ICBM programs. By the late 1960s, the United States had developed the Safeguard system based on the Sprint and Spartan interceptor missiles and the Soviet Union first the Griffon and then the Galosh system. All systems rely on radar to locate and track the incoming RVs and to direct the ABM to the intercept point. Neither the American nor the Soviet efforts would have been

World War III probably will see two major military interactions – the confrontation of the ICBM forces of the two superpowers and the land battle in Europe, where NATO and the Warsaw Pact have now amassed the most formidable concentration of military power in history. The two opposing politico-military coalitions in Europe, which arose after World War II, are based on the perceived military threat of the other. While there would almost certainly be major land fighting in the Far East, pitting Soviet firepower against Chinese manpower, Europe, and particularly Central Europe, is where the United States/NATO and the USSR/Warsaw Pact have concentrated the bulk of their forces. The battle in Europe will be a high-stakes' game indeed, because the prize is mastery of Western Europe with its rich industrial and population resources.

If World War III should break out, the West Europeans are probably in the least enviable position of all. The United States and USSR face nuclear attack on their homelands which probably will be highly destructive in physical and human terms. The East European allies of the USSR face heavy conventional attack and probably nuclear strikes also, but little actual combat on their territory. The West Europeans, on the other hand, face being both the central conventional and nuclear battlegrounds and possible occupation by Warsaw Pact forces. The West European states would thus become part of the Soviet bloc as did the states of Eastern Europe after World War II. The Soviets have done their best to ensure that Western Europe will in fact be the battleground by deploying large numbers of troops on the territory of the East European allies. One lesson the Soviets have drawn from the German invasion in World War II is never again to permit the battle to be fought on their territory. The positioning of their forces in Eastern Europe serves the dual purpose of enforcing the subservience of their allies and marking the boundary be-

Overleaf: German mobile rocket launchers take part in the annual Reforger exercises on NATO's central front in West Germany.

Above: the West German Leopard II (illustrated), together with the US Abrams M-1 and Soviet T-72, are the main battle tanks of the 1980s.

tween Eastern and Western Europe as the battle line.

The force postures and military strategies of the two coalitions have changed considerably over the past three decades. In the early days of the Alliance, NATO planners envisioned a purely conventional defense and aimed to have 96 divisions deployed in 1952. Since that time, however, the force goals have dwindled in the face of reliance on tactical nuclear weapons and improved weapons' technology and modernization. By 1961 the force objective was only 28 divisions, but Europe was considered secure, with the NATO tactical nuclear superiority and the unquestioned strategic superiority of the United States serving as effective deterrents to Soviet aggression. Once the growth of the Soviet ICBM force raised the specter of the destruction of the United States as well as the Soviet homelands, the entire military picture for NATO began to change. It is now thought that a war could occur in which conventional and tactical nuclear combat took place in Europe without involving the strategic arsenals of the superpowers. War in Europe thus has three possible dimensions – conventional, tactical nuclear and strategic nuclear – which could occur either sequentially or simultaneously. Since 1967 NATO has officially maintained a policy of flexible response which calls for conventional forces able to provide a range of options during crises and capable of preventing local Soviet adventures. Once Soviet intentions for serious aggression have been made manifest, however, the planned NATO response is an escalation of force to whatever level, including major nuclear warfare, is necessary to thwart Soviet aims.

The Soviet Union has also gone through an evolution of force posture and strategy. Emerging from World War II with very large theater forces, Stalin used these to hold Europe hostage as a counterweight to United States strategic power. In the mid and late 1950s the Soviets were able to add a powerful nuclear-strike capability against Europe through deployment of large medium-range bomber and missile forces. The Soviets also deployed tactical nuclear weapons, but until recently were sharply inferior to NATO in this area. Soviet doctrine proved as susceptible as that of NATO to reliance on nuclear weapons. As a result, the Soviet Union departed from its historic reliance on large ground forces and heavy conventional firepower and gave the primary role in theater war to nuclear weapons. In the late 1960s the

Left: the common origins of the Abrams M-1 (illustrated) and the Leopard II are betrayed by their remarkably similar appearance.

doctrine will surely continue to develop as their own and NATO forces change. Soviet use of nuclear weapons in the theater has been, and will probably continue to be, governed by the given situation and military expediency.

It is difficult to compare the relative military strengths of the two alliances because their force structures are very different. The main areas of current deployment and presumed future conflict are central and northern Europe. Here the authoritative *Military Balance* reports that some 27 NATO divisions face around 46 Warsaw Pact divisions, of which 26 are crack Soviet units. A United States Army division comprises 16,000 men and other NATO divisions are almost as large, but Warsaw Pact divisions have only between 10–12,500 men. Overall estimates of ground-forces' manpower give the Warsaw Pact perhaps a 50–60 percent edge. Another

Soviet Union, like NATO, began to change its view of war in Europe and to explore possibilities other than immediate large-scale nuclear warfare. Since that time Soviet theater forces have expanded in size. They have adopted more flexible doctrines and have equipment capable of coping with a variety of both nuclear and non-nuclear contingencies.

Soviet doctrine is still strongly nuclear oriented, because the Soviet Union still clearly expects any large-scale military conflict to involve widespread use of nuclear weapons. Soviet writings retain a consistent emphasis on the timely use of nuclear weapons, even to the point of preemptive strikes, but

Below: the Soviet T-72 medium tank is lighter by comparison to its Western competitors, but is nevertheless a very effective weapon.

important item of comparison is the tank. NATO has 7000 main battle tanks in operational service and another 1200 French tanks would probably be committed to NATO in wartime. The Warsaw Pact has 19,500 tanks, of which 12,500 are Soviet. While NATO is clearly outmatched in these measures, it does still maintain a considerable superiority in tactical nuclear warheads (7000 versus 3500) and in the long-range deep-strike capability of its tactical air forces. These static comparisons reveal important differencies, but there is no way to measure many other factors such as training, morale, leadership, tactical initiative, flexibility, geography and even luck. Nor can other intangibles such as the reliability of the Soviet Union's East European allies really be known before the event.

Left: Soviet T-64 tanks undertake a river crossing, one of the most difficult military operations, while MiG-23s fly overhead.

NATO's numerical disadvantages must also be weighed against the plans and circumstances of each side. NATO's plans strongly emphasize the defensive, while those of the Warsaw Pact are strongly focussed on the offensive. There are various defensive options open to NATO planners such as making a spoiling offensive to disrupt the attack preparations of the enemy or maintaining a defensive shield behind which a counteroffensive could be prepared. Yet a third possibility is a fixed, linear frontier defense, but military history shows that this is usually a recipe for disaster. Defenses must rather be organized in depth, have some elasticity and maintain some reserves to make local counterattacks until a major counteroffensive can be prepared.

However, NATO's planning for

Right: an M-48 tank of the US 3rd Armored Division advances toward an objective during field training in West Germany.

Above: US troops undergo realistic training exercises with M-60 tanks at Fort Carson, Co.

Above: Soviet T-55 tanks advance under cover of smoke with infantry in support during Warsaw Pact maneuvers.

defense is determined by political circumstances rather than these time-honored military principles. The Atlantic Alliance's strategy is to avoid war through deterrence. Public opinion of its members' countries requires that its defense policies show no aggressive intent whatever. Political realities in both the United States and Western Europe limit the resources available and thus leave NATO lacking the forces necessary to mount a major counter-offensive or even restorative counter-attacks. An elastic defense in depth which traded territory for time would require initially yielding up much of West Germany, the most powerful of the European members of NATO, and then returning to use it as a major, probably nuclear, battleground. Political necessity has thus forced NATO to adopt a rigid linear defense on the eastern border of West Germany lack-

ing both depth and substantial reserves.

Although this politically dictated defense strategy violates classic military principles, it cannot be condemned outright. NATO's goal is to deter Soviet aggression, not to destroy Soviet war-making capability. In war the strategy is to mount a stubborn forward defense and respond flexibly by countering Soviet moves at whatever level they are mounted. NATO plans to use its superior weaponry and high firepower to exact the maximum cost and force the largest delay possible on the attacker, to prevent the Soviet Union from gaining its objectives quickly and, if possible, to force the war into a conventional stalemate. This would give NATO time to bring its superior manpower and military-economic resources to bear, particularly reinforcements from the United States and the full commitment of French forces, which it is believed would join those of NATO. It would also raise the possibility of ending the war through negotiation, which both sides might well find

preferable to continuing the combat. The major NATO assumption is that a Warsaw Pact attack of whatever size will be conventional and can be constrained by conventional response. A second major (and perhaps dubious) assumption is that the first use of nuclear weapons will rest with NATO.

The Soviet approach is diametrically opposed to that forced upon NATO by circumstances. The Soviets believe that the outcome of wars turn on decisive offensive actions which destroy the enemy forces, liquidate the opposing government and occupy its territory. The Soviet Union believes that the best defense is to attack and destroy your enemy, which allows the time and point of attack to be controlled. 'The object of the offensive' according to one recent Soviet writer, 'is total defeat of the enemy. . . . It is achieved through competent use of all weapons, through the use of all forms of fire and through decisive actions of all the troops. . . . Fire is the principal resource for annihilating the enemy in battle.' The Soviet objective is to break the NATO defense quickly by marshalling superior forces at given points and then sending powerfull armored forces through the breaks to crash into the rear areas of the defense. The Soviets contend that total victory can only be achieved by the maximum application of force.

The land battle in Europe will be a complex operation for both sides, involving the close coordination of various interdependent force elements and weapons systems. The focal point will be the tank but it will need support, for both sides agree that the tank cannot have free run of the battlefield. The tank is at the heart of the land threat of the Warsaw Pact but is also vital to the defenders. The Soviets believe that land warfare in the west will be a series of encounter battles between highly mobile forces on battlefields of great depth lacking clearly defined front lines. In such circumstances only armored forces can be decisive and then only if supported by armored infantry and mobile artillery and air defense. NATO has developed an antitank-oriented defense, with some reliance on antitank guided missiles, but is also modernizing its own tank force. NATO is thus concerned with halting Warsaw Pact armored thrusts. The Warsaw Pact is concerned with suppressing the antitank-oriented defenses of NATO to achieve the breakthroughs necessary.

As a weapons system the tank has revolutionized warfare by combining mobility and armored protection with the firepower of the cannon. This revolution was not at all evident, however, when the tank made its first appearance on the battlefield at the Somme in 1916. As its tactical employment had yet to be thought through, the tank did not break the stalemate on the Western Front as many had hoped. In the interwar period a number of theorists thought that the tank would return mobility and maneuver to warfare – J F C Fuller and B H Liddell Hart in Britain, Charles de Gaulle in France, Heinz Guderian in Germany and Marshal M N Tukhachevsky in the USSR.

The tank came of age as a tool of war in World War II, especially in the German and Soviet armed forces. Although the Treaty of Versailles

Above: an M-60 tank of the US 3rd Infantry Division moves across snow-covered terrain on winter training in West Germany in 1977.

banned German tank manufacture, the Germans developed a range of machines in the 1930s and during the war. The Soviets developed the very influential T-34 mounting a gun with good antitank performance but also able to fire high-explosive shells against soft targets. The T-34 was rugged, reasonably mobile and offered relatively good frontal protection because of its well-shaped armor. The qualities of the T-34 were such that the Soviets gained a whole generation lead in tank development. The United States and Britain, on the other hand, built tanks, often with high silhouettes and inadequate gun power, nowhere near comparable to the German panzers or the Soviet T-34. Even so, World War II tank operations were often governed by high-velocity towed or self-propelled antitank guns. Later in the war, the infantry gained real antitank weapons in the recoilless rifle, bazooka and Panzerfaust, firing ammunition with shaped-charge warheads. Tanks were also vulnerable to low-level air attack. As the war progressed, the combatants found it increasingly necessary to add more and more infantry and artillery support to their tanks. A strong school of thought even held that the tank was hopelessly vulnerable before its array of enemies.

In the postwar period, improved firepower and design brought the tank back both as an offensive and defensive weapon, as the prowess of the improved T-34s in Korea in 1950 demonstrated. The American M-26 Pershing was also well able to hold its own in this period. In the early 1950s, the French pioneered a new generation of antitank missiles which again caused analysts to say obsequies for the tank. This second generation of antitank weapons made the tank again seem vulnerable to its enemies, but recently the tank has been given a new lease of life. The British have developed compound or 'Chobham' armor (named after the Military Research Center at Chobham, Surrey) which greatly improves the tank's ability to withstand the projectiles of infantry antitank weapons. The Chobham-armored tank still has a welded-steel shell for structural strength and general protection, but the high vulnerability areas of the hull front, and front and sides of the turret are fitted with compound-armor packs. These packs give good protection with acceptable weight and size and can be changed to meet different forms of attack. This notable advance has been shared with the United States and West Germany and it can be assumed that the Soviets have something comparable by now.

There are several types of compound armor. Light-alloy honeycomb armor is a series of layered hexagonal cells which spread the jet of gasses formed by the shaped-charge (or HEAT) shell and thus considerably degrade its effectiveness. This type of armor is most common on light-armored vehicles rather than main battle tanks. Compound armor of the British Chobham type has three layers: an outer one of armor steel, a middle of ceramic honeycomb and an inner one of aluminum alloy. Such armor is carried by the US Abrams, German Leopard II and probably the new Soviet T-80 tanks. Coupled with other improvements, the new armor technology has made the tank again the dominant variable in the battlefield equation, at least until anti-tank technology moves forward in response, as it may already be doing.

A major method of attacking tanks is with 'high-explosive antitank' (HEAT) rounds. These are termed shaped explosive charges and have been in existence since World War II. When the shell explodes on the armor surface, a high-temperature jet of gasses burns through the armor like a cutting torch and affects the interior of the tank with its remaining energy. The French SS-11 wire-guided antitank missile is the first important example in the postwar period but within 10 years all antitank guided missiles (ATGMs) were employing shaped-charge warheads. Compound armor reduces HEAT effectiveness against the main parts of the tank. Only the roof of the tank is probably still vulnerable, and it will only be hit when weapons are fired from above.

The principal shell fired by tank guns is the kinetic energy (KE) type, which concentrates the maximum energy of the shell against the smallest possible area of armor in the hope of breaking through and in the process taking a lot of armor material with it. KE rounds have a high lethality because of the amount of metal they inject into the interior of the tank. In the future the most common KE round will be the 'armor-piercing discarding-sabot fin-stabilized' (APDSFS) round. Such

rounds are far more efficient when fired from a smoothbore rather than a rifled gun. Needless to say, ATGMs cannot use KE rounds because they do not have the velocity and hence cannot transmit the requisite energy to the tank. Compound armor is more susceptible to KE than HEAT attack and thus the primary antitank weapon against it is the high-performance gun.

Modern fire-control systems employ laser rangefinders and digital computers to achieve very high first-round-hit probabilities and a large increase in effective range. The newest tanks have suspension systems making them fairly agile and mobile across country. They are thus able to reduce their periods of medium and high risk by laying the gun while still in motion and moving with the sight laid. The new United States Abrams tank can direct rapid accurate fire at its targets while doing 45mph across somewhat rough terrain. Its predecessor, the M-60, can do 12mph across similar terrain. Compound armor has brought kinetic attack back to the fore but effective HEAT attack will probably reappear in the next round of the armor/antiarmor technological contest.

It is generally agreed that for the foreseeable future the main battle tank will remain the primary weapons system in nonnuclear mechanized warfare. The laser rangefinder has revolutionized gunnery, especially tank-against-tank, by giving up to 80 percent first-round hits at 4500 meters. In addition to its offensive roles, the main battle tank with its KE armament is a far more effective antitank weapon than the current ground antitank weapons because its relatively small size, mobility and protection make it a difficult target. Brigadier Richard Simpkin, a leading student of tank warfare, has written 'I most seriously doubt whether any conventional modern tank, even with compound armor, could sustain a hit at

Below: the M-48 main battle tank is still in widespread service in NATO and the US has some 4000 for the Army Reserve and National Guard.

short or medium range from a 120mm or 125mm APDSFS projectile and remain fit to take part in the battle.' In the 1980s, according to Simpkin, the only fully effective antitank weapon system will be the antitank gun with the KE round.

Modern tanks have been improved in many ways other than their protection. The silhouette has generally been lowered on Western tanks, but the Soviets have always preferred squat models. One recent improvement has been variable suspension systems which raise and lower the hull between the tracks. This innovation makes it easier to adopt a hull-down position while preserving cross-country mobility. Such suspensions are already found on the Abrams tank and reportedly on the T-80 (although if this vehicle includes everything that has been reported about it, it will truly be a wonder tank). Suspension also helps to improve mobility which has been limited in earlier tanks because of weight. Current tanks employ a very powerful engine, or sometimes more than one, with usually a moderate reduction in armor in order to be 'extremely lively.' The view now seems to be that mobility and single-shot kill capability are better protection than thicker armor.

Tanks are making more active use of camouflage. They can throw out their own smokescreens within one or two seconds by means of externally mounted smoke canisters to blind optically guided ATGMs. Chemicals can be added to the smoke to distort electronic sensors. The tank can simulate the infrared signature of vegetation with certain types of infrared reflective paints, while other paints absorb radar waves to degrade targeting by radar.

Tank survivability has been further enhanced by improved ammunition storage and fuel protection and better compartmentalization and fire-suppression systems. In some cases engines have been moved forward to improve crew survivability in the event of frontal hits. The rear can then be used for larger amounts of fuel and ammunition and for crew escape under fire if need be. Tanks have nuclear-bacteriological-chemical (NBC) systems to defend against such attack. By maintaining the

internal air pressure slightly higher than atmospheric and filtering all air, contaminants can be held at bay. However, these systems are not so effective that the crew members do not have to wear individual protective gear. This requirement apparently contributes to crew fatigue but does not seriously detract from performance. In nuclear situations, both conventional and compound armor will eliminate alpha and beta radiation and markedly attenuate gamma radiation but do not offer much protection against neutrons which is why the neutron bomb is considered an effective tank killer. The only recourse against neutron weapons would be to fit the crew compartment with a boronated polymer liner, which is feasible in terms of weight and space but to my knowledge has yet to be done for any tank.

Tank firepower has undergone marked changes. Main battle tanks now mount 115mm to 125mm main guns except for the United States M-60 and Abrams tanks. Although initially produced with a 105mm gun, the Abrams will be retrofitted with a 120mm gun in 1948. West Germany and the Soviet Union have adopted the smoothbore gun to which the United States is now committed in principle if not yet in practice. The move away from rifled barrels stems from the fact that spin tends to reduce penetration by diffusing the HEAT jet. Range and accuracy on fin-stabilized rounds are also reduced by spin. Smoothbores also weigh less, give less recoil and do not wear out as rapidly as rifled tubes. The disadvantages are that smoothbores give shorter range and cannot fire all ammunition types. Fin-stabilized KE rounds with discarding sabots to increase muzzle velocity and maintain velocity along the projectile trajectory are now standard. Improved rounds are now being developed to increase penetration. The United States, for example, is testing a KE round with a tip of depleted uranium whose heavy mass is intended to aid penetration. Laser rangefinders, computerized laying of the gun and

Right: an M-60A1 tank with the M-239 smoke-grenade launcher mounted on the turret. Smoke can defeat optically guided ATGMs.

gyro-stabilization are becoming standard. The more advanced tanks use light intensification and passive infrared devices for more effective night operations.

Like so many other aspects of the combatants' arsenals, the tank forces in the field will range from the models of the 1950s to the new supertanks of the early 1980s. Tank arsenals on both sides are currently in a cycle of major modernization which will last well into the latter part of the decade. Designing and introducing a new main battle tank, however, is not a task to be lightly undertaken. New tanks are very expensive and development cycles run around 10 years in most cases. The strategy adopted by most countries has been to modernize models already in produc-

tion. The French, West Germans and Americans have all had success with this approach with the AMX-30, Leopard I and M-60. Much of the improvement is now in such areas as ammunition, fire-control systems and stabilization which can be installed on existing models and prolong service life by many years. From an economic standpoint, this is important because main battle tanks such as the AMX-30, Leopard II and Abrams are extremely expensive, the latter costing over $1,000,000 each. Budgetary constraints can thus limit procurement and force substantial reliance on improved older models. There are also those who question whether the technological supertanks are even worth it. Brigadier Simpkin says, 'The superior tank will

very rarely be able to exploit all aspects of its superiority at once and will not often be able to exploit even one of them fully. Most of the time, the inferior tank would do the job just as well.'

The Soviet Union has evolved its operational and tactical doctrine around the tank and has always 'fielded very sound tanks with a design balance suited to their concepts and a level of complexity suited to their crews.' The tank force on which the Soviet Army bases its strategy includes two generations. It is believed that a number of World War II T-34s are stockpiled in the depots of the USSR and its allies. The succeeding T-54/T-55 series probably is still the most widely used tank in the Warsaw Pact. It is good basic hardware, once

described as being built like a 'super-heavy tractor,' and is reasonably well armed, protected and mobile. The Soviet Union apparently planned to upgrade its force with the T-62, which went into production in 1961 with a longer, wider hull and larger gun. The tank was the core of Egyptian and Syrian armor in 1973, but it was found to have a slow rate of fire and an inadequate fire-control system. It is considered distinctly inferior to its United States contemporary, the M-60, by western analysts. The T-62 ceased production some years ago but is still in service with Soviet forces.

In the 1970s, the Soviet Union fielded an entirely new family of tanks in the T-64 and T-72, and the T-80 is expected soon. The design of the T-55/T-62

family labelled them as primarily 'break-through tanks,' but the newer family has a notable tank-fighting capability and is thought to reflect the lessons of the Middle East wars and the prospect of major tank battles in Europe. The T-64 can compete with the Leopard I, M-60 and British Chieftain, while the T-72 would be only a little overmatched by the Leopard II and Abrams. The T-80 is not believed to be a completely new design but an improved T-72, well able to compete with the best Western tanks.

Right: Soviet T-64 tanks carry out maneuvers. The T-64 and T-72 began to replace the earlier T-55 in Soviet armored units during the 1970s.

Below and bottom: Soviet T-62 tanks carry out training exercises. The 40-ton T-62 is being gradually supplanted by the newer T-64 and T-72.

The Soviet ground forces are so large and require so many tanks, however, that modernization proceeds only slowly. The T-80 will probably not be a significant factor during the 1980s, owing to lack of numbers. The best tanks NATO will face will be the T-64 and T-72 which will gradually take over the force from the T-55.

The most important NATO tank is the Leopard I, with some 4500 in service with seven armies, a testament to enduring German skills in tank design. After the reestablishment of the German Armed Forces in the mid-1950s, the first armored force consisted of 1000 M-47 and M-48 tanks. The

Right: NATO forces carry out maneuvers in 1979. The flags on vehicles indicate those which have been adjudged casualties in the exercise.

Below: the Soviet 122mm self-propelled howitzer is an amphibious vehicle, weighing less than 16 tons. The gun can fire five rounds per minute.

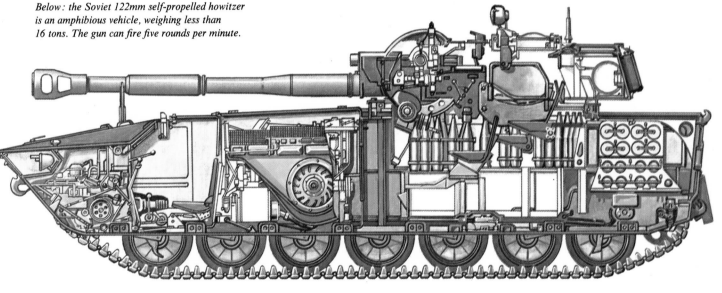

Below: a cutaway illustration of a T-62 tank adapted from a Soviet military magazine. The T-62 weighs 40 tons and mounts a 115mm gun.

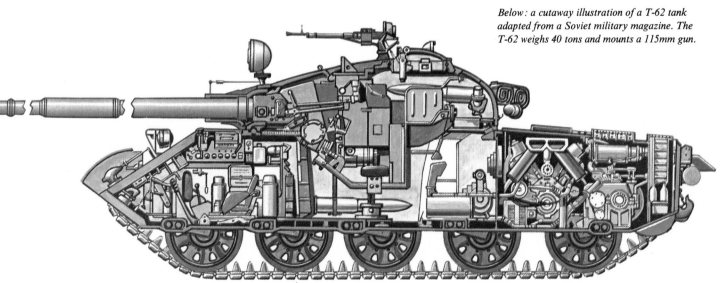

Leopard had its origins in a joint Franco-German venture to develop a new battle tank but each country soon went its own way. The French produced the AMX-30, still in production, while the Germans developed the Leopard, which was what the French called the German result of the joint venture. With its superior firepower and mobility, the Leopard was the best Western tank and remained in production until 1979. It is in service with the West German, Dutch, Belgian, Danish, Norwegian, Italian, Canadian, Australian and (soon) Turkish forces. Over the years, it has been upgraded with better fire control, protection and stabilization.

The new German tank, the Leopard II, went into series production in 1979. It also originated in a failed joint venture with the United States which has produced the remarkably similar Abrams tank. The Leopard II is scheduled to replace the M-48 as the Leopard I replaced the M-47s. The West Germans plan to procure 1800 Leopard IIs by 1986 and the Dutch have ordered another 445 units. Beginning in the mid-1980s the Germans plan to replace the Leopard I with the Leopard III which has been under development since 1972. Concept development was carried out in conjunction with the British who are developing a new tank as well.

With 8500 M-60 and 1800 M-48 tanks of various models, the United States has the largest number of tanks next to the USSR. The M-48 was in production from 1951 to 1959 and almost 12,000 were produced. Improvements were made along the way, including, on some models, the same gun and engine as the M-60. The M-48 saw extensive service in Vietnam, but it is now used primarily by the National Guard. The M-60 entered production in 1960 with an M-48 hull and turret but with a British 105mm gun and a new diesel engine. A variant termed the M-60A2 was developed with a new turret mounting a 152mm gun/missile launcher called the Shillelagh. It was not a successful experiment as the missiles were expensive and have a slower rate of fire and time to target which leaves the tank vulnerable. Production will continue into the early 1980s with the improved M-60A3 carrying the same laser rangefinder and 105mm gun as current Abrams production models. The M-60 has been a reliable and effective weapons system, but has only seen service with United States and Israeli forces. The other members of NATO have preferred the Leopard I.

The Abrams tank has been under development since 1971 when the German-American effort to produce a joint main battle tank foundered on differing views and high costs. Over 7000 Abrams tanks will be procured by the end of 1987. Early production models mount a 105mm gun, but the United States is committed in principle to installing the 120mm smoothbore carried by the German and Dutch versions of the Leopard II. The tank is fitted with Chobham armor and a turbine rather than a diesel engine. The latter has been a controversial design decision and some experts believe that a second generation of tank turbine technology is necessary before this type of engine, attractive because of its light weight and simplicity of maintenance, can reliably replace the diesel. The Abrams is the first completely new American battle tank since the end of World War II and will represent a major step up in the effectiveness of the US Army's armor. The Abrams tank does not, however, represent the latest in tank technology by any means. It is, as one officer told the author, rather the best technology that the money available will buy.

The British and French have a different time scale in developing a new main battle tank compared to the Americans, West Germans and Soviet Union. The current British and French tanks are the Chieftain and the AMX-30, contemporaries of the Leopard I and the M-60. The Chieftain has more armor protection and a heavier gun than any of its contemporaries but for a long time had a weak engine for its size. No other country in Europe uses the Chieftain. The majority of the 800

Chieftains are in service with the British Army of the Rhine. The British are now at the point where decisions on replacing the Chieftain must be made. A new tank with Chobham armor, 120mm rifled gun, advanced diesel engine and laser rangefinder is being designed and the first production models are scheduled for 1989. The Chieftain will thus remain in service until the mid-1990s or later. The French had planned to develop a new tank, the AMX-32, but have decided instead to upgrade the AMX-30 which emphasizes firepower and mobility at the expense of some protection.

The 1980s will thus see major improvements in the tank forces of NATO and the Warsaw Pact. Strong modern tank forces are vital to NATO for political as well as military reasons. Former British Minister of Defense Denis Healey once described the tank as the 'symbol of virility' of modern armies and that is largely true. Like the ICBM for the United States and USSR,

the tank is a symbol of national power and purpose and the centerpiece of NATO's conventional deterrent. Tanks are also the primary weapons system by which modern armies are judged. Much of the perceived Soviet military threat to Western Europe derives from the size and power of the Soviet armored forces.

However powerful and technologically sophisticated they may be, even the new supertanks are not self-sufficient on the modern high-intensity battlefield such as Central Europe promises to be. This is especially true for the offensive. Thus both sides have fielded complex families of specialized vehicles to support the tank in its battlefield roles. This in turn has made coordination of tactical forces on the battlefield more complex. Support forces consist of infantry combat vehicles, self-propelled artillery, and self-propelled antiaircraft guns and SAMs.

'In the legs lies the whole secret of maneuver and battle' wrote Marshal de Saxe in the eighteenth century. This is more true than ever. As offensive tactics are more and more concentrated on the tank, the infantry must also have mobility to keep up and help protect the tank from its many enemies. This mobility has been provided by the armored personnel carrier (APC) which is now giving way to the mechanized infantry combat vehicle (MICV). The APC is a lightly armored tracked or wheeled vehicle designed to move personnel, usually a squad of infantry, quickly into battle with a modicum of protection from shrapnel and small-arms fire. The infantry has always been the most exposed and vulnerable element in battle and has borne the heaviest casualties as a result. This has been especially true since the advent of mechanized firepower in the twentieth century. The horrendous infantry casualties of World War I on the Western Front led to the first attempt at an APC, the British-designed Mark IX tank with a capacity for 40 soldiers. Perhaps fortunately, this monster was

Left: a West German Leopard tank participates in the annual Reforger exercise. This involves the reinforcement of NATO forces from the US.

not tested in battle before the war ended.

APCs were widely used in World War II. The Germans and Americans employed half-tracks, the SdKfz 251 and M-3 respectively. The British and Canadians removed the turret from the Ram tank (Canadian version of the M-4 Sherman) and the Ram Kangaroo APC resulted, which had essentially the same armor and mobility as the tank with which it served. Since the war half-tracks have almost disappeared and APCs are usually wheeled or fully-tracked. The best examples of wheeled APCs are the highly successful British Saracen and the Soviet BTR series. The standard APC outside the Soviet bloc is the American M-113 tracked APC which has been a very reliable and successful vehicle, seeing extensive service in Vietnam. Since entering service in 1964, over 64,000 M-113s have been built. Other tracked APCs are the British FV-432 and French AMX-VCI.

The APC has evolved from being merely a 'battlefield taxi' to a weapons platform and fighting vehicle in its own right. The Soviets led the way with the BMP, first seen in 1967, and the first MICV. This vehicle was designed specifically to operate in NBC environments for exploitation of tactical nuclear strikes in conjunction with tanks. Able to carry eight soldiers in addition to its crew of three, the BMP has firepower equivalent to a light tank: a 73mm gun, a coaxially mounted 7.62mm machine gun, a Sagger antitank missile, and firing ports for the infantry passengers. It is also fully amphibious. The BMP has been the envy of many Western military men as it greatly adds to the offensive potential of a Soviet motorized rifle division or tank division.

The first Western MICV is the very sophisticated and very expensive West German Marder. Production began in 1969 and stopped after 3000 units were built. The Marder carries a crew of four together with six infantry and is armed with a 20mm cannon and two 7.62mm machine guns. It is not amphibious. The United States has experimented with several MICVs, one of which has been adopted by the Dutch. The MICVs presently under consideration are the XM-2 infantry fighting vehicle and the

XM-3 cavalry fighting vehicle. These have been criticized as not meeting operational requirements and being too costly, causing Congress to balk at funding significant procurement and leaving the United States forces still buying the M-113. The British are also facing decisions on replacement of the FV-432 but no plan has yet emerged. The French are replacing the AMX-VCI with the AMX-10P armed with a 20mm cannon.

Operational requirements for MICVs are different for NATO and the Warsaw Pact. As the presumed aggressor, the Warsaw Pact will use its tanks as the lead element, supported by armored infantry, artillery, helicopters and tactical air support in a highly mobile tactical battle that has ill-defined boundaries. The infantry must keep up with the tanks to deal with the antitank defenses and pockets of resistance which have been by-passed or overrun. The infantry must also occupy and secure terrain which the tanks have overrun. For the defense, the primary task of the MICV would appear to be to move infantry rapidly from one defensive

Left: the US M-2 infantry fighting vehicle is a replacement for the trusty M-113. It mounts a 25mm cannon and TOW ATGM launchers.

Below: troops advance after disembarking from M-113 armored personnel carriers, when practicing squad tactics at the US Army Training Center.

Left: a US soldier in NBC protective clothing washes an M-113 APC during an exercise dealing with chemical-warfare attacks.

position to another, while adding their weapons to the general antitank and anti-MICV defense. For both sides, however, the MICV is expensive and increasingly sophisticated, adding yet another set of maintenance problems in the field. A MICV-mounted infantry battalion in the 1980s will thus be a very costly proposition.

The infantryman has been equipped with high-firepower automatic rifles for many years. Since 1953 most NATO members have used the Belgian-designed FAL (Fusil Automatique/Léger) 7.62mm rifle which currently is in service in some 70 countries. The FAL is unquestionably the most successful and widely used infantry rifle in the post-World War II period. Its closest rival is perhaps the sturdy Soviet 7.62mm AK-47 (Kalashnikov) which entered service at about the same time. An estimated 25,000,000 AK-47s have been produced. The AK-47 is a simple and reliable weapon which can take a lot of abuse and still work in the field. This is in marked contrast to the American M-16, which had early problems in the field but has now been improved. The M-16 is a light weapon firing a 5.56mm (.223 caliber) bullet which tumbles on impact and 'goes in small but comes out large.' The Soviets

Left: US troops dismount from an M-113 APC. One of the most widely used APCs, the M-113 can carry 11 infantry plus two crewmen.

Left: the BTR-60PB is the standard Soviet wheeled APC. It carries 14 soldiers, plus two crew, and mounts two machine guns.

have begun to introduce the AK-74, a lighter version of the AK-47, which fires a 5.45mm bullet. NATO is also considering adopting a 5.56mm rifle in the 1980s but may opt for an even smaller caliber, such as 4.7mm, since the 5.56mm technology is already outdated.

Artillery has been the greatest producer of casualties in war in the twentieth century. After a long period when missiles and nuclear weapons were considered the primary means of firepower on the battlefield, artillery is now enjoying something of a renaissance because it still offers levels of accuracy, reliability, durability and economy yet to be matched by any other mass strike

Left: the BMD is the airborne version of the Soviet BMP infantry combat vehicle and mounts the same 73mm gun and Sagger ATGW.

Below: Soviet troops dismount from BMP infantry combat vehicles during training. The BMP is amphibious and carries eight soldiers.

Above: the US M-16 rifle, pictured in action in Vietnam, is a light weapon firing a 5.6mm bullet which tumbles on impact.

weapon. The guns themselves have changed little since World War II, but developments in ammunition and fire control have brought great strides in effectiveness and versatility. The other important trend is a movement toward self-propelled pieces.

Artillery did not change from the end of World War II to the early 1960s as both NATO and the Warsaw Pact tended to emphasize nuclear rather than conventional firepower. Indeed, large amounts of artillery were withdrawn from the Soviet forces in this period. In the early 1960s, the United States began to redesign its World War II equipment with the Kennedy-

MacNamara reorganization of defense policy. Shells were reengineered to obtain maximum range and destructive power. Known as 'upgunning,' the process has made the 105mm howitzer as effective as the 155mm gun of World War II and Korea. Artillery had been mounted on tank chassis in World War II to allow fire support to keep up with the fast pace of armored offensives. The United States began to introduce a new family of self-propelled guns in the early 1960s. The advantage of self-propelled guns is their quicker reaction time. While the 8-inch self-propelled gun cannot fire on the move, it can open fire about one minute after it stops moving, whereas a towed piece takes a good half hour to set up. The smaller self-propelled pieces offer some crew protection by enclosing the crew in

what is essentially an iron box, but the larger American guns do not.

Artillery falls into the two broad categories of close and general support. Missions are broadly interdiction, meaning action against rear areas and second echelons, and direct fire support of combat units in the front lines. In general support, artillery predominates up to around 30km while missiles and rockets predominate beyond that point. In recent years artillerymen have experimented with even longer ranges through new high-energy propellants and rocket-assisted projectiles, but apparently they are having some problems with reduced accuracy and payload, wear and tear on the tube and blast overpressures on the crew. There are still strong arguments in favor of longer ranges which enable the guns to move less while covering

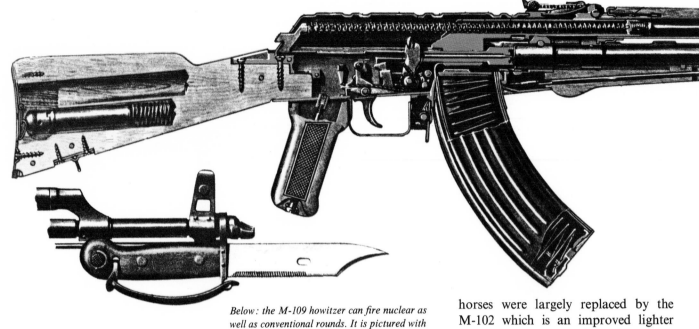

Below: the M-109 howitzer can fire nuclear as well as conventional rounds. It is pictured with an M-548 cargo carrier.

horses were largely replaced by the M-102 which is an improved lighter version. These two pieces have been versatile and reliable performers, able to fire high-explosive, smoke and hollow charge shells and various antipersonnel weapons such as the M-546 carrying 8000 flechettes and the M-413 and M-444 which dispense small antipersonnel grenades.

High priority is now being given to improved conventional munitions (ICMs). These are essentially cargo-carrying artillery shells which dispense submunitions or sensors. One such shell carries 88 miniature dual-purpose shaped-charge mines which are effective against light armor, soft vehicles and

more of the length and depth of the battle.

The standard United States general-support guns are the M-107 175mm, the M-109 155mm, and the M-110 8inch (203mm). All three are more capable, self-propelled and they all entered service in 1962. All of these guns are in common use in NATO, but the main general-support weapon is the 155mm. The larger guns are now considered to be unnecessary because their ranges are covered by missiles. The M-107 never was very satisfactory and is being withdrawn from service to be upgunned to 8-inch status. Improved versions of the M-110 will remain in service. In the 155mm group, the M-109 is also being improved and the M-198 towed version is entering service. This last will be the

standard piece of the direct-support artillery battalions of light divisions and corps general-support battalions. Britain, West Germany and Italy have jointly produced a new 155mm piece, termed the SP-70 in its self-propelled version and the FH-70 as a towed weapon, which is now entering service. The French have also developed their new TR 155mm gun. All of these towed weapons have auxiliary propulsion which enables the gun to have limited mobility without its prime mover.

The 105mm gun is the standard close-support weapon. The United States M-101A1 was produced from 1937–53 and, as one authority noted, is 'probably the world's most ubiquitous artillery piece, having been supplied to nearly 50 countries.' In the mid-1960s these work-

Above: the Soviet AK-47 (Kalashnikov) automatic rifle is a simple and reliable weapon.

Right: the US M-110A2 eight-inch self-propelled howitzer has a maximum range of 26,000 meters.

Below right: a US 155mm towed howitzer is shown in action in Vietnam in 1965.

personnel. Another carries nine magnetically fused antiarmor mines capable of stopping any current tank. Unless detonated, the mines self-destruct after a certain period of time. It is thus possible for artillery to sow instant antiarmor and antipersonnel minefields before, behind, and beside the enemy, a new capability which could have a major impact on the course of the land battle.

There are many variants of these ICMs, some of which are terminally guided. The 155mm Copperhead M-712 cannon-launched guided projectile uses a laser seeker to home in on the laser light reflected from the target after it has been designated by a nearby team

Below: a field-artillery command post is pictured with 175mm self-propelled guns in the firing position during the Vietnam War in 1966.

Above: men of the US 25th Infantry Division fire a 105mm howitzer in support of operations near Pleiku, South Vietnam.

either on the ground or from an aerial platform such as a helicopter. A similar weapon is the STAFF (smart, target-activated fire-and-forget) 155mm shell which uses a very small antenna in its nose to measure the radio waves bouncing off the metal of the target. STAFF only needs to be fired in the general direction of the target, after which a small onboard computer guides the projectile. Both the Copperhead and STAFF were designed specifically for use against Warsaw Pact armor formations in Central Europe.

NATO guns are in general well-proven designs with good fire-control and target-acquisition systems. They are, as Ian Hogg has observed, inferior to the Warsaw Pact only in quantity. The main differences are that the Warsaw Pact has substantially larger numbers of guns and substantially smaller numbers of self-propelled pieces. The standard artillery weapons in Soviet divisions are the D-20 152mm

and D-74 122mm howitzers which have both towed and self-propelled versions. Self-propelled guns are being introduced slowly in the 122mm, 152mm and 203mm sizes. The Soviets have also upgunned their ammunition and developed ICMs but are not known to have any terminally guided artillery munitions as yet. With an historic penchant for massed artillery fire to breach enemy defenses, Soviet doctrine requires large numbers of guns to suppress enemy antitank and air defenses before the main armor assault. Tanks must be supported by artillery, preferably artillery that can move with them as they breakthrough – hence the Soviet trend toward self-propelled guns.

NATO's rationale for self-propelled artillery is survivability through mobility or 'shoot and scoot' as dictated by counterbattery fire. One important difference between NATO and Warsaw Pact artillery is that the new NATO guns are, in the words of Ian Hogg, 'complicated and expensive weapons which have to be supported by fire-control systems and information-

gathering systems which threaten to become a tail bigger than the dog.' If the Warsaw Pact does have an advantage in artillery it may be its large numbers of basic towed pieces.

Both sides also use unguided rockets to supplement cannon artillery in heavy combat. Massed rocket attack has played an important role in the Soviet doctrine of heavy firepower since World

War II and the 'Stalin organs.' The Soviets have a number of weapons in their inventory but the most common is probably the 122mm, 40-tube, truck-mounted BM-21 which has a reload time of 10 minutes and a range of around 20km. NATO is fielding a far more potent weapon, the general-support rocket system which is a cooperative development of the United States, West Germany, Britain and France. A tracked launcher will be able to single or ripple fire 12 solid-fuel rockets with a maximum range of more than 18 miles in less than a minute. The system will be incorporated into both division and corps artillery for close-support and interdiction roles. The 12 rockets among them can place 8000 M-42 submunitions, each about as destructive as a hand grenade and able to penetrate light armor, in an area the size of six football fields. Each rocket can be individually aimed and is believed to be more accurate than any existing free-rocket system. It is intended to give NATO quick heavy firepower against surging Warsaw Pact forces. It can also deliver the German AT-11 scatterable antitank mine and thus further complements the ICMs of the artillery.

The type of conventional fire represented by the rifle, machine gun, artillery and free-flight rocket has probably reached its definitive form. While im-

Above: a Soviet 122mm BM-21 multiple-rocket launcher was photographed during a military parade in Moscow.

provements will continue, the limitation will always be the ammunition supply. The cost of ammunition and the nature of the targets requires carefully controlled shots with higher kill probabilities rather than massed area bombardment. The tank and APC/ICV can pass through unguided fire with only random chance of hits. Another separate category of weapon, the anti-tank guided missile (ATGM), has been developed specifically to counter the sophisticated armor of the 1980s.

The ATGM basically evolved from the World War II bazooka. This simple weapon involved one man with a shoulder tube firing a small fin-stabil-

ized rocket with a shaped-charge warhead. The hit probability was very low, but even so this rudimentary weapon gave the infantry the means to protect itself, and when present in numbers seriously constrained certain tank tactics. When rudimentary command guidance was married to this weapon, the modern ATGM was born. The first generation ATGMs use command guidance via a wire trailing from the missile toward a target which must remain in the operator's sight the entire time.

Below: Soviet troops exercise with 122mm M-30 howitzers. This weapon is a standard divisional artillery piece.

Above: the Multiple Launch Rocket System can launch 12 230mm free-flight rockets singly or in a ripple-fire sequence.

Earlier models required the gunner to keep the target in the crosshairs of the sight and guide the missile with a joy stick but later models with semiautomatic guidance require only that the crosshairs remain on target and the system does the rest.

Most of the ATGMs currently in the field are first generation systems and have at best a 50 percent single-shot hit probability. They have many drawbacks, however, which can reduce their effectiveness substantially. Target acquisition is the key to ATGM

Left: the Soviet BM-21 rocket launcher carries 40 122mm rockets with a range of over 20,000 meters. The weapon is truck-mounted.

Right and below right: the M-47 Dragon medium antitank missile can be carried and fired by one soldier. It is a wire-guided weapon.

effectiveness. All current systems require clear sight of the target and thus are vulnerable to smoke, dust, darkness, bad weather and effective use of terrain by the intended target. Indeed the ATGM has given new importance to tank maneuverability and speed, clearly reflected in the design of the T-72. The ATGM also has a slow rate of fire and the gunner must remain in position during the entire time of flight to the target. In that space of time, the target can move to cover and/or open fire on the gunner whose position has been revealed. The tank can fire 10–12 rounds per minute while the ATGM gunner can only fire one or two rounds per minute. There is also the question of how many reloads the ATGM launcher will have available and thus of its staying power in a major engagement.

The standard NATO ATGMs are the Milan (used by Britain, West Germany and France), the Mamba, Dragon, Swingfire and the TOW (tube launched, optically tracked, wire-guided). These can be mounted on helicopters, jeeps, and modified APCs, or be deployed with crews of foot soldiers. A new generation of ATGMs is now appearing. These are 'fire-and-forget' weapons that break the physical connection between the gunner and the missile by using laser seekers to home in on laser spots on the target. A designator other than the gunner can maintain the spot, leaving the latter free to 'shoot and scoot' or engage another target. Typical of these missiles is the Hellfire, the projected replacement for the TOW.

The Soviet Union is fully aware of ATGM development and has fielded its own family of these weapons, the best known of which is the Sagger, which is mounted on a number of mobile and airborne platforms. The Soviet Union sees the ATGM as an important factor in the battle but believes that it cannot be the determining factor even for an

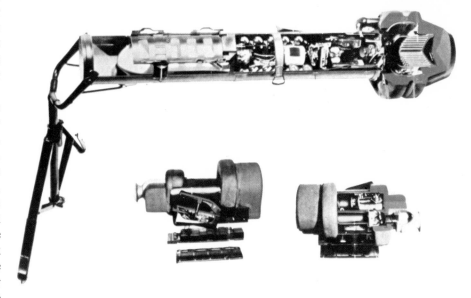

Right: the TOW ATGM is one of the most important NATO weapons in the battle against Soviet armor.

Above: a Soviet FROG (Free Rocket Over Ground) on its transporter-erector-launcher is in the ready to launch status.

ATGM-oriented defense because of technical and operational limitations. ATGMs are very vulnerable to artillery fire, hence the main Soviet response is to suppress them with preparatory barrages since their likely positions can be deduced from their known ranges and other factors. The Soviet Union has also developed tactics for the engagement of ATGMs by tanks on the battlefield. These include maintenance of movement and speed, full use of masking agents such as smoke, terrain and vegetation, and the broadcast of short warnings from one tank to others to trigger specific and immediate responses.

While the war remains conventional, the main battle will focus on the forward edge of the battle area (FEBA), a zone of distributed defenses comprising minefields, antitank positions, artillery and tanks to a depth of many kilometers. The offense will try to develop its attack, taking into consideration advantages in terrain, the distribution of enemy strength and possibilities for

tactical surprise, and then concentrate its forces to gain at least a three to one (and preferably much larger) local advantage. When the opposing lines are not strong or uniform, tank-led forces can break through and envelop the defenses from the rear. However, when the defense is in depth with no apparent weak spots, it must be suppressed by heavy artillery barrages and air attacks, then dismounted infantry supported by fire from its ICVs and artillery must attack the surviving points in the defense, especially the antitank positions. The battle will probably now mostly consist of many small, company to regimental size, unit actions taking place simultaneously. It may take several waves of attacks by the infantry to suppress the defenses but only then can the armor pass through (by-passing as necessary still-active points of resistance) to disrupt the enemy rear and attack his flanks. If the defender has tank reserves (as he should), these will at this point challenge the penetrating armor in an engagement well behind the FEBA. Depending on the terrain and degree of urbanization, this could be a classic tank battle such as Kursk or the Sinai in which the opposing tank

forces shoot it out in a mass action or it could be more diffuse with other second echelon forces of the defender joining in.

A well-executed and supported armored attack on the model above is a powerful action indeed. The Warsaw Pact has the necessary forces to mount such an attack, but a properly organized defense, making use of terrain, mines, antitank weapons and tanks themselves, can counter it. Any factor which slows up the tempo of the offensive contributes to the defense by fixing the attackers and exposing them to greater rates of attrition. It may in fact require repeated barrages and waves of infantry and ICVs to crack the defenses, during which the waiting armor is exposed to air, artillery and long-range missile attack. The ATGMs may well tip the loss ratios somewhat in favor of the defense, but both sides will unquestionably suffer very heavy losses when all the available firepower is unleashed.

Once the offensive in Central Europe has begun, a number of outcomes can be conjectured, but most point toward the nuclear threshold. If the offensive succeeds and NATO finds its back to the wall, its policy is to consider going nuclear. If the offensive fails to breach the defenses and stalemate develops, the two sides may decide to negotiate or the Warsaw Pact may decide to blow holes in the defense with its plentiful supply of nuclear weapons and accept the outcome of NATO nuclear retaliation. If the offensive fails and NATO mounts a successful counterattack, the Warsaw Pact would probably resort to nuclear weapons to prevent its own defeat. This last is an unlikely scenario, however, since no serious observer credits NATO with the capability to mount a serious counteroffensive, nor is such a course declared NATO policy.

If it is difficult to imagine the outcome of a conventional war in Europe with all our accumulated historical experience with that type of war, how much more so with theater nuclear war with which we have no experience at all. Yet both sides are very well equipped with battlefield and 'Eurostrategic' nuclear weapons which place all of Europe, including the western part of the USSR, at heavy risk. Any conventional war in Europe will take place under the ultimate threat of the resort to nuclear weapons. The United States and NATO do not have a real doctrine for the use of nuclear weapons in the theater, only guidelines on conditions permitting or preventing use. The procedural and political problems associated with these weapons have obscured the very real military problems in their use. We do not know what Soviet doctrine may be, but Soviet use will at least not be indiscriminate according to Soviet writers. Colonel Shirokov has written that 'The objective is not to turn the large economic and industrial regions into a heap of ruins . . . but to deliver strikes which will destroy strategic combat means, paralyze enemy military production, . . . and sharply reduce the enemy capability to conduct (nuclear) strikes.'

The amount of civil, as opposed to military, damage would be immense in a nuclear war in Europe. Europeans tend to see in this the main deterrent against war breaking out and have thus preferred strong nuclear forces over strong conventional defenses. The damage would not be limited to Western Europe but would extend to Eastern Europe and probably the USSR. A

Above: FROG-7 rockets are mounted on Zil-135 trucks. The FROG can carry nuclear, chemical, or high-explosive warheads over 70,000 meters.

large enough Soviet nuclear attack would probably provoke the United States and NATO into massive strikes on the USSR proper. Human response as individuals and in groups on the battlefield to nuclear weapons is simply not known. Many military men believe that even a small nuclear exchange involving a few dozen weapons, let alone the thousands which paper exercises employ, might well render the majority of troops either unable or unwilling to continue.

Battlefield nuclear weapons are generally short-range missiles or air-delivered bombs which are designed to attack primarily second echelon forces. The missiles, such as the Soviet Scud B and the United States Lance and Pershing 1A, have guidance systems while the Soviet free rocket over ground (FROG) does not. Close support is offered on the NATO side by 155mm and 8-inch guns which can fire nuclear shells but the Soviet Union is also believed to have nuclear-capable artillery. Short-range missiles lack the accuracy of guns and are too expensive and in too short supply to launch without good targets. Thus air-delivered weapons have some advantages, but are slower to target and vulnerable to enemy defenses.

Behind the battlefield weapons stand the so-called 'Eurostrategic' missiles and bomber aircraft, which are termed long-range theater nuclear forces (LRTNF). While NATO has had a strong advantage in tactical nuclear weapons until very recently, the Soviet Union has had a longstanding and sizable edge in LRTNF. Soviet capabilities were based on the Tu-16 Badger and Tu-22 Blinder medium bomber forces and the SS-4 and SS-5 missile forces deployed in the western USSR. In recent years, the bomber and missile forces have been modernized with the Tu-22M Backfire

Below: a Soviet SS-4 medium-range ballistic missile rises into the air. Over 500 of these early missiles were deployed.

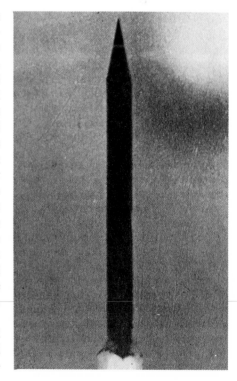

Top: the Soviet SS-12 Scaleboard is a medium-range 'Eurostrategic' nuclear missile.

Above: the SS-5 intermediate-range ballistic missile has a range of over 2000 miles and a one-megaton warhead. The aged SS-5 is also part of the early Soviet nuclear threat to Western Europe. Its successor is the new SS-20.

Right: an SS-4 MRBM lifts off a soft launch pad. These missiles have been the core of the Soviet nuclear threat to Europe since the 1950s.

Above left: the US Pershing II intermediate-range ballistic missile is scheduled for deployment in Europe in 1983.

Above: the Pershing 1A battlefield support missile has been a NATO theater-strike weapon since the late 1960s, 108 being deployed.

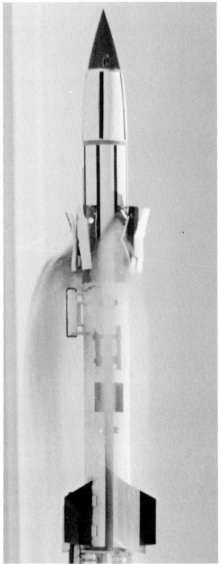

Left: the T-22 corps-support system is intended to replace the Lance battlefield missile. It is powered by a solid-propellant rocket motor.

Above: the T-22 can carry a nuclear warhead, or perform the conventional antitank mission by dispensing a large number of guided submunitions.

bomber and the SS-20 mobile missile, which give the Soviet Union more effective, survivable and flexible weapons for the theater. NATO has relied on quick-reaction aircraft – RAF Vulcan and USAF F-111 bombers – and the missiles of the British and part of the United States ballistic missile submarine forces. NATO has not deployed land-based missiles with range enough to strike the USSR proper since the late 1950s and early 1960s. In 1983, however, NATO is scheduled to deploy

Above: the US Army's Night Vision Sight can detect enemy activity in faint skyglow, moonlight, or starlight at 1200 meters' range.

Right: a soldier and tank stand out clearly when viewed through a Night Vision Sight.

108 Pershing II ballistic missiles and 464 ground-launched cruise missiles (GLCM) which can cover a wide range of targets in the western USSR. Each weapon is highly effective but the small numbers planned make them more of a symbolic contribution to NATO's deterrent than a major military contribution to NATO's defense.

In the days of massive retaliation, Europe was protected from Soviet aggression by the threat of American strategic retaliation. As United States strategic forces began to grow vulnerable in the face of the Soviet strategic buildup and as the United States began to emphasize 'flexible options' as a policy, Europeans increasingly worried that the American nuclear umbrella was leaking badly. They worried that United States strategic forces would not necessarily be used in the defense of

Europe at the risk of a retaliatory Soviet attack on the United States. First Britain and then France developed nuclear forces to serve as independent deterrents to the Soviets. Nuclear attack on either country will unleash these weapons on Soviet cities. The British maintain bombers and submarine-based missiles, and the French have bombers, missile submarines and land-based missiles.

The nuclear equation in Europe is thus complex and not completely under the control of either NATO or the Warsaw Pact. Few observers believe that the land battle in Europe can remain at the conventional level, but that sooner or later one side will feel forced by military circumstances to cross the nuclear threshold and so open the Pandora's box of nuclear war with all its unknowns.

7:THE WAR IN THE AIR

Air-power enthusiasts since Giulio Douhet and General Billy Mitchell have argued that the aircraft could be the determining factor in warfare through strategic bombardment and its ability to attack ships and thus dominate the use of naval forces. In World War I the aircraft was used primarily for observation, but as the war progressed a struggle for local air superiority also developed to protect the reconnaissance aircraft. Toward the end of the war, the strategic bomer finally made its appearance. The Germans bombed both Paris and London and the British prepared a counterstrike against Berlin.

The aircraft played major tactical and strategic roles in World War II. It had a wide impact on the battlefield as it provided fire support on demand and could attack the second echelon levels and logistics in interdiction roles. The naval war in the Pacific hinged largely on naval air power. The aircraft enabled the Germans to mount a destructive but militarily ineffective 'blitz' against Britain early in the war. The German bomber force was not optimized for strategic bombardment, however, and was later joined by the V1 and V2 missile barrage, itself no more effective. The Allies in turn devastated Germany and Japan with their powerful fleets of long-range, heavy-payload bombers. Although highly destructive, it is questionable what contribution such attacks made to the military defeat of the Axis powers.

Since the simple biplanes of World War I, aircraft design has advanced rapidly. A large armada of heavy bombers, light bombers, close-support aircraft, interceptors and highly specialized reconnaissance and command and control planes has developed. To counter this array, a formidable group of strategic and battlefield air defenses has appeared and promises to make air combat in a future war exceptionally intense. In the European theater, NATO relies heavily on air power for close support and interdiction against the larger Warsaw Pact ground forces. The Warsaw Pact in turn has fielded a dense array of ground-based air defenses and made important strides toward improving its tactical air forces. The long-range bomber has lost the central role in strategic bombardment to the long-range missile, but it is making a comeback through new technological developments.

There are four main operational missions for theater tactical air forces: reconnaissance, close air support, interdiction and counterair. There is considerable overlap among these missions as most planes can perform several or all of them.

Reconnaissance provides information on the disposition, composition and movement of forces, locations of installations such as command posts and ammunition and fuel dumps, and lines of communication. Aircraft will also help to establish the enemy's electronic order of battle by forcing him to turn on his equipment and monitoring the emissions. Poststrike coverage of air and artillery strikes to establish the degree of target damage, weather, terrain and battle surveillance with 'real-time' reporting are other important aspects of tactical reconnaissance. Timely information is now considered to be the key factor in successfully co-

Overleaf: a McDonnell-Douglas F-15 Eagle air superiority fighter launches an AIM-7F Sparrow air-to-air missile.

Above left: a weapons specialist prepares Sparrow missiles for loading onto a USAF McDonnell-Douglas F-4 Phantom.

Left: members of a USAF munitions maintenance squadron arm an F-4 fighter. The F-4 can carry four AIM-7 and four AIM-9 air-to-air missiles.

ordinating the diverse elements of both offense and defense on the modern battlefield.

Tactical aircraft are too few in number and too expensive to be launched on random searches for targets in the battle area. Tactical air defenses have become too effective to risk in reconnaissance the reduced numbers of aerial platforms available which are much more effective in weapons delivery roles. Manned reconnaissance and the Forward Air Controller concept are being reduced in emphasis in favor of remotely piloted vehicles (RPVs). These very small unmanned aircraft can degrade enemy radar networks by serving as jamming and chaff-dispensing platforms. They can also penetrate enemy airspace to alert electronic systems so these can be located and attacked. The ultimate RPV is both a sensor and weapons system. Strike RPVs locate their targets such as radars, SAMs, command and control facilities, and airfields and, rather than relaying data for use by other strike systems, perform the attack themselves. The United States prototype RPV is only six and a

half feet long with 13-foot wingspan which gives it virtually no radar signature.

As reconnaissance platforms, RPVs are equipped with television cameras and other sensors which transmit real-time data back to forward air-control parties at the lowest command level and behind these direct air-support centers. These centers coordinate local air-support and air-defense operations. Reconnaissance data thus feeds into a complex, computerized command and control system which is part of the trend toward battlefield automation. These systems are vulnerable to degradation and even elimination through direct attack. As one experienced combat officer noted, 'Once the real shooting starts, I don't think it will be long before we are back to plastic map overlays and grease pencils.' Both sides still widely use fixed-wing reconnaissance platforms with longer range sensors.

Close air support aircraft attack first-echelon forces, those in close proximity to one's own forces. Air attacks against ground targets are complex operations requiring extensive communications

Above: F-15As painted in the air superiority 'ghost grey' color scheme. The F-15 is the most technologically advanced fighter now in service.

and theater-wide coordination in many cases. Tactical aircraft are still the most flexible means of bringing heavy firepower to bear at short notice at disparate locations and thus enable the attack or defense to be shifted rapidly. Long-range artillery cannot perform this function nearly as effectively because of range and deliverable payload limitations. Nor can missiles, unless they employ nuclear warheads.

Several important trends can be seen in close air support. Until recent years, the United States and NATO countries had a strong preference for multi-purpose aircraft which combined ground-attack and counterair capabilities. Largely due to the constraints of cost, the United States in particular produced relatively large, all-weather fighters and fighter-bombers which, through sophisticated avionics, were highly flexible operationally. The F-104, F-4, F-5 and F-15 are all multirole aircraft, as is the new trinational Tornado in Europe. The trend has been partly reversed with the advent of the F-16 and F-18. Even these, although optimized for the interceptor role, were designed for air-to-ground capability as well.

NATO is now further enhancing its close air support capabilities by developing a specialized combination of aircraft and helicopters which are solely designed for this mission. The first of these craft is the V/STOL (vertical/short takeoff and landing) Harrier, which does not require a conventional operating base. This is highly desirable because the airfields of both sides are considered prime targets for sustained attack, which means that conventional takeoff aircraft will have to stage farther to the rear. The Harrier is also extremely agile and can probably outmaneuver any enemy aircraft. Early United States and West German attempts to produce V/STOL aircraft failed, so the Harrier is the only such aircraft available to NATO. It has been in service with the RAF since 1969 and with the US Marines since 1971. The Soviet Union has a V/STOL aircraft in the Yak-36 Forger, but it has only seen service aboard the two Soviet aircraft carriers *Kiev* and *Minsk*. It is a low-performance aircraft held in low regard by western analysts except for its V/STOL technology. There is a strong school of thought which holds that the V/STOL aircraft is the machine of the future in the European theater because it is difficult to locate, provides quick response to requests for close air support and is capable of sustained independent action.

The USAF contribution to dedicated fixed-wing close air support is the A-10, an ungainly-looking beast nicknamed the 'warthog.' It is designed exclusively for low-level operations against ground targets, especially Warsaw Pact armor, and can carry 10 types of bombs and missiles. Its most formidable weapon, however, is a seven-barrel gatling gun in its nose. This 'tank buster' unleashes 4200 rounds per minute at very high velocity. A burst from this weapon transmits tremendous kinetic energy to the target and can literally 'puree' any tank currently on the battlefield. Slower than a conventional jet fighter, the A-10 can make tighter turns and stay longer over the battlefield. It will be forced to

Right: an A-10 close-support aircraft is pictured with a typical ordnance load. Its 30mm GAU-8A cannon fires up to 4200 rpm.

operate in a very hostile environment and will be a prime target for the Soviet radar controlled ZSU-23-4 AA gun. The A-10 has thus been fitted with AA-radar-jamming equipment and is designed to absorb considerable damage, keep flying and be easily repairable.

The A-10 is intended to operate in conjunction with attack helicopters which, over the last 15 years or so, have become mainstays of the ground-support mission for both NATO and the

Below: an artist's conception of the A-10 in action against enemy armor. This is the aircraft's principal role in Central Europe.

Warsaw Pact. Helicopters have been in service since World War II for observation, liaison, medical evacuation and transport services. It was not until Vietnam that the helicopter really came into its own as a combat aircraft. One major innovation was the total integration of helicopters into the Air Cavalry Brigade, thus making them the prime means of mobility for a major ground formation. An even more important innovation was the armed helicopter, which first had machine guns on flexible mountings and rocket launchers. As the offensive requirement increased, the AH-1G Cobra gunship

was developed as a relatively simple and inexpensive variant of the standard UH-1 'Huey' transport.

After Vietnam, where the orientation was primarily antipersonnel, the combat role of the helicopter was focussed on the antitank problem in Central Europe. There the helicopter has the same virtues as the Harrier in that it does not need fixed bases, which can be located and attacked. The helicopter can quickly concentrate a high volume of antitank fire at threatened points in the defense. It can for example deal with enemy armored spearheads and airborne landings and generally harass the enemy. As a highly maneuverable craft, the helicopter can travel close to the ground, taking advantage of the terrain for cover but not being impeded by it, launch ATGMs at the enemy up to three kilometers distant, and resume cover. It is thus a highly mobile platform for the ATGM, a fact which has encouraged NATO to plan for over 2000 of these craft by the mid-1980s.

For all its virtues, however, the helicopter can only complement rather than form the main antitank defense. It cannot really stand and fight on its own, because it is a fragile aircraft with little direct protection. Once detected the

Below: the AH-1 Cobra is the standard US gunship helicopter and will remain so through the 1980s. Here an AH-1G flies a training sortie in S Korea.

helicopter is highly vulnerable to AA fire and tactical SAMs. The United States lost over 4000 helicopters in Vietnam where there was no true tactical air-defense capability. Apart from the American experience in Vietnam and the USSR's operations in Afghanistan, helicopters have never been tested as combat systems and have yet to confront a true air-defense capability. It is still an open question as to how survivable helicopters will prove to be in the sophisticated high-intensity battlefield environment of the FEBA in Central Europe. The helicopter should be safe from fixed-wing aircraft, which would find it hard to attack the agile helicopter at heights of 200 meters and below. Efforts are being made to reduce the radar and infrared signatures of helicopters as well as to give them 'redundant' engines, fuel and oil supplies, and electrical systems.

The advent of the combat helicopter has opened up a whole new area of combat at 200 meters and below over the forward battlefield, a sphere which the Warsaw Pact has embraced as fully as NATO. Following the same pattern as the United States (and Britain and France), the Soviet Union began to add first machine guns, rocket pods, and then the ubiquitous Sagger ATGM to transport helicopters in the mid-1960s. From these grew specialized gunships – especially the Mi-24 Hind which has become the standard Soviet attack helicopter and is playing such a prominent role in Afghanistan. The Hind D version is armed with four rocket pods, two ATGM launchers and a four-barrel gatling gun in a chin mounting. It can carry eight passengers. It is a formidable and effective weapons system which, many analysts believe, has no equal in the NATO arsenal, at least until the US Army's new YAH-64 advanced attack helicopter reaches the field a few years hence.

Soviet interest in the combat helicopter is less for its specific antitank role than for its antitank defense-suppression capability and airborne assault potential. Gunships like the Hind can provide the close support needed by Warsaw Pact armored infantry engaging NATO forward defenses and can also support the fast-moving armored spearheads that the

Below: the Soviet Mi-24 Hind helicopter is used for combat assault and fire support and is armed with a cannon, Sagger ATGMs and rockets.

Right: a USAF F-4 launches a GBU-15 precision-guided glide bomb. Such weapons have markedly improved the effectiveness of air attack.

Soviet Union hopes will be the decisive element of the battle. Heliborne troops could be landed in the rear of NATO defenses and at other key points to perform the traditional role of para-troops. It has also been reported that the Hind undertakes antihelicopter and air-defense suppression roles.

A last important trend in close air support and ground attack has been the widespread introduction of the airborne PGM, usually referred to as air-to-ground (AGM) or air-to-surface (ASM) missiles. While the speed, range and payload of ground-attack aircraft have all been improved over the years, the main problem has always been the inaccuracy in delivering the payload on target. This inaccuracy stems from ballistic dispersion of free-fall ('iron') bombs, aiming errors, windage, and errors in computing the location and velocity of the aircraft in relation to the target. Indeed, bombing accuracy in actual combat has been shown to be several times lower than that achieved on the target range. Various technical

Below: the Hughes YAH-64 Advanced Attack Helicopter armed with advanced Hellfire ATGWs is being developed for service with the US Army.

solutions have been advanced such as image intensifiers and infrared (heat sensing) devices but all have proved to be really no more accurate than visual bombing.

Airborne precision-guided munitions (PGM), on the other hand, have brought new dimensions of lethality and surviva-bility to air-to-ground attack. Using laser and electro-optical guidance systems, the PGM's accuracy has greatly expanded the destructiveness of the attack and thus reduced the sorties per

target. As PGMs are usually launched at some distance from the target area, they reduce the exposure time of their platform to the enemy defenses and thus reduce vulnerability. This is becoming more and more important as air defenses continue to proliferate in the battle and rear areas.

The long-range or deep-interdiction mission is also important to each side. Soviet lines of communication reach from the western USSR across Poland to East Germany and Czechoslovakia,

while NATO's rear comprises eastern France, the Benelux countries and Britain. NATO's airborne deep-interdiction capabilities rest with the British Vulcan bomber force and two wings of USAF F-111s based in Britain since 1971. The delta-wing Vulcan first entered service with the RAF in 1957 and 48 are still in service in the strike role, but they are scheduled for retirement beginning in 1981. They will be replaced by the interdiction-strike version of the Tornado fighter-bomber. The Vulcan B2 has a range of around 4600 miles and carried standoff missiles until the mid-1960s. At that time, they were switched to low-level missions with iron bombs or nuclear weapons.

The newer F-111 went into service in the late 1960s after a more than controversial early career as the TFX – the plane that was to fulfill all functions in all services but did not. The F-111 was originally intended as an all weather, VG (variable geometry wing or 'swing wing'), long-range (2500 miles unrefuelled) fighter-bomber. It successfully flew low-level attacks against North Vietnamese targets and now performs close-support roles because it can carry a large ordnance load and stage out of its less vulnerable bases in Britain. The

Above right and right: the variable geometry wing General Dynamics F-111 serves as an all-weather fighter-bomber with the USAF.

Below: the Tu-16 medium-range bomber, code named Badger by NATO, has been a longlived and very successful design for the Soviet Union.

Below: the Tu-22 Blinder was the first Soviet operational supersonic bomber. Only about 250 were produced and some 130 remain in service.

Above: the Tu-16 has been the mainstay of Soviet Long Range Aviation and Naval Aviation since its introduction in 1954.

Vulcan and F-111 play central roles in NATO's theater nuclear deterrent.

Soviet missions against deep theater targets can be flown by the elderly Tu-16 Badger and Tu-22 Blinder and the new Tu-22M Backfire bombers. The first two are old designs which are being replaced by the Backfire. An estimated 2000 Badgers were produced for Long Range Aviation and Naval Aviation after 1956 and as many as half of these are thought to be still in service. The several strike versions can carry iron or nuclear bombs or several different ASMs. Several other versions have reconnaissance or electronic-warfare

Below: a US Navy F-4 fighter-interceptor launches a Sparrow III, an early air-to-air missile with precision radar guidance.

Bottom left: the MiG-21 is still the most widely used combat aircraft in the world. Many version have appeared since the first in 1955.

missions. The range is about 4000 miles. The Blinder was the first Soviet attempt at a supersonic bomber, but it is thought to have been a basically unsatisfactory venture for the Soviet Union, because of its disappointing 1400-mile range. Until the advent of the Backfire in the mid-1970s, the Soviet Union relied on the workhorse Badger, once aptly described as 'a good basic airframe endlessly adapted to meet new requirements and carry new equipment.' The medium-range bomber force is now being modernized with the Backfire, a VG mach 2 (at high altitude) strike aircraft, whose range may be as much as 5000 miles. It can carry iron and nuclear bombs and an ASM. The Backfire greatly increases Soviet capabilities to carry out deep-strike missions in the intense air-defense environment of western Europe.

Between the close air support and deep-interdiction aircraft, both sides have a number of conventional fighter-bombers. The workhorses of the Soviet fighter-bomber force are turning out to be the MiG-27 Flogger D and the Su-17 Fitter C/D. The first modern Soviet aircraft designed specifically for interdiction is apparently the Su-24 Fencer, a somewhat mysterious plane that western analysts have yet to get a good look at. The Flogger and Fencer are modern-generation designs and the Fitter is not too far behind. All are VG aircraft which are capable of carrying iron and nuclear bombs as well as ASMs. NATO relies on the older F-104, F-4, Jaguar and Mirage V. Its modernization program is focussed on the F-15, F-16 and Tornado.

Counterair encompasses missions against enemy combat aircraft, airfields and air-defense sites. It also involves what are now called 'air-superiority fighters' and ground-based gun and SAM defenses. Again there is considerable disparity between NATO and Warsaw Pact forces. NATO has fewer, but notably better, interceptors and fewer ground-based air defenses (which are now being modernized). NATO also has notably superior air-to-air missiles. Until the 1970s the Warsaw Pact did not emphasize the conventional ground-attack mission, but has always fielded large numbers of tactical and strategic air-defense fighters to complement its long-standing emphasis on strong ground-based air defenses. NATO has relied more heavily on high-performance fighters than ground defenses. The battle in the air is important because control of tactical airspace is essential to the tactical and operational mobility of both offense and defense.

Until the mid-1960s the Soviet Union fielded short-range interceptors, of which the MiG-21 Fishbed has been the most widely deployed. The design of the early models of this small aircraft was strongly influenced by the jet-versus-jet combat of the Korean War. Over the years the MiG-21 has been so 'product improved' that the most recent variants are almost regarded as new types. In the late 1960s the MiG-23 Flogger B made its appearance armed with air-to-air missiles and a 23mm cannon. It was followed by the MiG-25 Foxbat which

has both air-defense and reconnaissance versions. The Flogger is becoming the mainstay of Soviet air defense and is roughly comparable in technology and operational capability to the NATO F-4 generation of aircraft. The Soviet Union is believed to be developing a new generation of air-superiority fighters, but it could be some years before these are available.

NATO is almost a generation ahead of the Warsaw Pact in fighters and ground-attack aircraft because the modernization cycles of the two alliances are not synchronized. NATO's new generation of aircraft include the American F-15, F-16, F-18 and the trinational Tornado as well as the French Mirage 2000. Whereas the

preceding F-4 generation, fielded during the 1960s, tended to rely on air-to-air missiles in aerial combat, the newer NATO and Soviet planes are again mounting guns and the NATO aircraft at least have greatly improved dog-fighting performance. The missile is still an important weapon of aerial combat at close range and is being used by stand-off air-defense interceptors, such as the Tornado ADV and the US Navy's F-14 with its AIM-54 Phoenix missile, at 130-mile range.

The air-defense mission is to protect forces and installations from direct air attack. Air defenses are usually layered, with radar-directed AA guns and man-portable SAMs providing battlefield air defense against helicopters and low-level attack, tactical SAMs against fighter-bombers and medium- and high-altitude SAMs giving area coverage of the rear areas. SAMs in particular have increased in effectiveness, making defense suppression the key element in the ability of air forces to carry out offensive missions. The Yom Kippur War of 1973 showed just how effectively

Left: Northrop F-5E Aggressors are used to simulate Soviet fighters as part of the USAF's fighter pilot training program.

Below: the MiG-21, code named Fishbed by NATO, is a short-range, clear-weather fighter. Later models have been extensively redesigned.

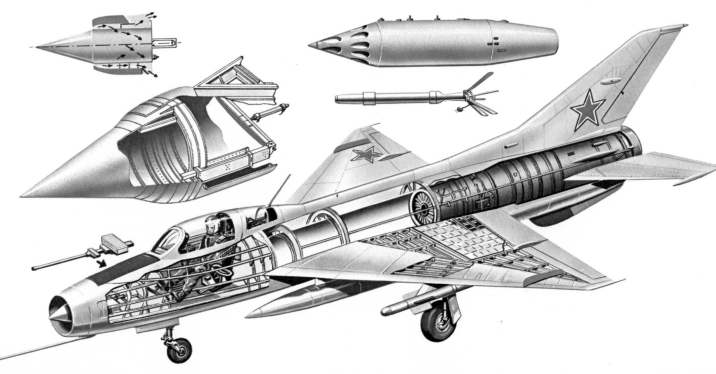

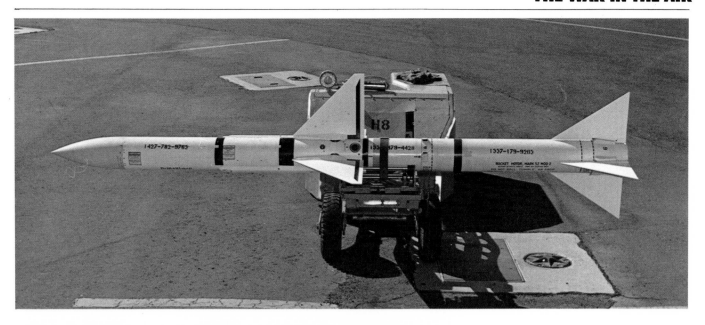

Above: the Raytheon AIM-7 Sparrow air-to-air radar-guided missile is an example of an early precision-guided munition.

Left: a close-up view of the missile armament of the General Dynamics YF-16, showing the wing-tip mounted AIM-9 and underwing AIM-7.

modern air defense can inhibit the fighter-bomber. Air forces are generally unwilling to accept rates of attrition of more than a few percent per sortie unless the objective is an extremely high-value target. The duel between the aircraft and the defender on the ground is thus forcing the former into more-costly and complicated responses, which divert planes from primary offensive missions.

The Warsaw Pact has a dense air-defense network consisting of long-range search radars, jamming units, fixed-site defenses and mobile defenses that move with the first-echelon ground forces. The infantry and armor protect themselves from low-level attack with shoulder-launched SA-7 SAMs and mobile ZSU-23-4 23mm quad-barrel AA guns which have proven their effectiveness in the Middle East wars. Behind these are the SA-6 and SA-8 mobile low-altitude SAMs and the SA-4 mobile high-altitude SAM. Fixed sites can mount SA-2 high-altitude and SA-3 medium-altitude SAMs. However, like all systems based on radar, the air

Left: the Soviet SA-7 SAM is a low-altitude, shoulder-launched weapon, which defends infantry from low-level air attack.

defenses are susceptible to jamming and deception by electronic counter-measures (ECM) and are vulnerable to attack once their locations are known. Attack can come from antiradiation missiles or guided missiles and bombs. Except for the newer tactical SAMs, Soviet SAMs also tend to be large and difficult to fire in quantity. A massed attack could saturate target-acquisition and tracking systems and rapidly expend available firepower. The Soviet Union has compensated for these weaknesses by fielding large numbers and has made its air defenses effective from sheer volume of fire.

NATO has a smaller but more advanced air-defense arsenal. Its SAMs have better guidance and thus better kill probability and are more resistant to ECM. Beyond that the two arsenals are fairly similar. NATO's shoulder-launched weapons are the United States Redeye (now being replaced by the Stinger) and the more capable British Blowpipe. Mobile radar-directed AA guns have been provided by the United States Vulcan, a daylight, fair-weather-only system, which will soon be replaced by the far more capable DIVision Air-Defense (DIVAD) system. The

Left: the Soviet SA-2 surface-to-air missile provides an effective defense against high-altitude bomber aircraft.

Below: SA-2 missiles were extensively used in the Vietnam War, where it required between 50–100 SA-2s to down one US aircraft.

Chaparral forward-area, low-altitude mobile SAM has been operating in conjunction with the Vulcan. Originally intended to be replaced by the Roland low-level all-weather SAM (being adopted by most NATO members), the Chaparral is being improved and retained in service as Roland procurement has been sharply cut due to high costs. Other low-level mobile systems in use are the British Rapier and the French Crotale. The low to medium-altitude Hawk has been a standard NATO SAM since the early 1960s, with an improved version deployed in the 1970s. It is scheduled to be replaced by the Patriot SAM in the 1980s. This last system is designed to counter high-speed aircraft and missiles at all altitudes and to be jam and ECM resistant.

While aircraft in the theater are playing increasingly complex roles, the intercontinental bomber has lost its primary role as the ultimate vehicle of cold-war deterrence to the ICBM and now plays essentially a tertiary role in strategic attack behind ICBMs and submarine-launched missiles. The Soviet Union never did develop a large or effective intercontinental bomber force, while the once mighty USAF bomber fleet can now most charitably be described as decrepit. Technology is, however, causing a revival of interest in the bomber, at least in the United States and the 1980s may see the beginnings of a somewhat revived bomber force.

The United States has a long tradition of building strategic bombers from the B-17 of the mid-1930s to the present long-lived B-52. The USSR, on the other hand, has yet to design a really successful intercontinental bomber and indeed has not fielded a design since the mid-1950s. At that time, the Soviet

Left: in service since 1960, the Hawk SAM is the main air-defense weapon in the US field forces. An improved Hawk was introduced in 1972.

Below: the US Army's Chaparral forward area air-defense missile entered service in 1969. It is an adaptation of the Navy's Sidewinder.

Below: the Patriot tactical air-defense system
will replace the Hawk in the 1980s. It is able to
function in the intense ECM environment
expected in the 1980s and 1990s.

Above: USAF Voodoo interceptors still form part of the small force of air-defense aircraft based in the United States. These include squadrons of the Air National Guard.

Right: the Nike-Hercules high-altitude SAM was phased out of the US defenses in the 1970s. A few units are operational abroad.

Union brought out the M-4 Bison with a 7000-mile range and the Tu-95 Bear with a 7800-mile range. The jet-engined Bison was not a successful design for its role and has become primarily a tanker for in-flight refuelling. The Bear has turboprop engines and has served very well as a long-range reconnaissance aircraft. As a strike weapon the Bear can carry conventional or nuclear free-fall bombs or ASMs. Neither the Bear nor the Bison was ever produced in quantity and only 43 Bisons and 113 Bears remained configured as bombers in 1980.

The Soviet intercontinental air threat is considered so small that the United States has not deployed SAM defenses for some years and has no new strategic SAMs under development. The USAF has no strategic interceptors under development, but it does still maintain a small force of air-defense interceptors, primarily the elderly F-101B Voodoo and the F-106A Delta Dart. These

could be supplemented with tactical aircraft, such as the F-15 and F-4, stationed in the United States if need be. Over the years the USSR has built formidable strategic air defenses based on an estimated 9000 SA-1, SA-2, SA-3 and SA-5 SAM launchers and an interceptor force of around 2600 aircraft. These forces came to offer such dense coverage at medium and high altitudes that the USAF switched its bomber tactics from high-altitude to low-level penetration. The Soviets are believed to be able to field new interceptors and a new SAM during the 1980s that will be more effective against low-level penetration, so the US is now considering switching more to standoff than to penetrating attack.

For almost 30 years the mainstay of the USAF bomber force has been the B-52. Originally designed to attack at 50,000 feet and above, the B-52 has effectively switched to tree-top-level tactics and shown itself capable of flying tactical-support missions in Vietnam as well. Yet the B-52 is an old aircraft. First flown in 1954, the last B-52 came off the production line in 1962. The supply of mass-produced parts has long since been exhausted and these must now be built to order at an incredible cost. The average age of the B-52 force is over 20 years which,

Top: the DEW Line still watches for Soviet air attack over the North Pole. This radar site is at Cambridge Bay, Canada.

Above: the DEW (Distant Early Warning) radar site at Dye Main in Canada comes under the joint Canadian-US NORAD command.

under Federal Aviation Administration rules, would class them as antiques.

Since the 1960s the bomber force has been one leg of the strategic triad on which United States strategic doctrine is based. Soviet strategic air defenses are now becoming so effective that penetration may soon become much too costly to remain a viable attack option. The development of the long-range cruise missile with extremely accurate guidance now offers the option of stand-off attack. Cruise missiles are the descendants of the German V1

missile, small pilotless jet aircraft which travel just above tree-top height. They are slow, travelling at about 550mph, but are highly accurate and virtually impossible to defend against because their very small radar cross sections and low-altitude flight almost defy current air-defense radars. The accuracy stems from guidance known as terrain contour matching (TERCOM). The guidance system is fed the known locations of the launch platform and the target just before launching. The flight path is preprogrammed. During the

Below: a USAF B-52, operating as a conventional bomber, releases a string of 51 750lb bombs onto a Viet Cong target in South Vietnam.

Bottom left: this Boeing B-52H strategic bomber is armed with AGM-69 SRAM missiles, carried on pylons under the wing.

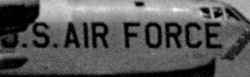

Below: an AGM-86B air-launched cruise missile drops from the weapons' bay of a Boeing B-52 strategic bomber during testing.

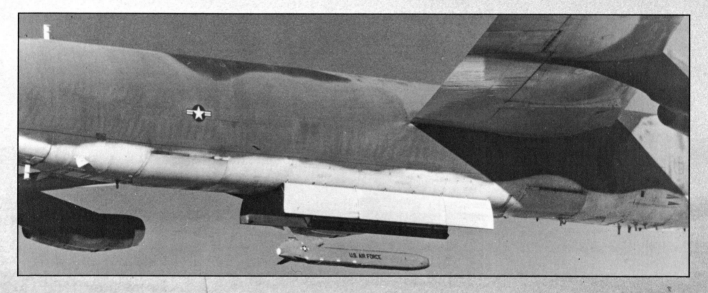

flight, the TERCOM equipment compares the terrain data stored in its computer with the altitude characteristics of preselected portions of the route obtained by a radar altimeter to confirm and adjust the missile's flight.

The disadvantage of the cruise missile is its slow flight time and inability to attack mobile or moving targets (but neither can any other long-range missile). However, they do not require elaborate launchers or bases and thus are difficult to destroy before launching. These marvels of small-jet-engine technology, solid-state electronics and advanced structures and dynamics promise radical change in both strategic

and tactical air attack. They are being developed in ground-, air- and sea-launched versions of varying ranges.

The major modernization program of USAF's Strategic Air Command (SAC) is the conversion of 173 B-52Gs to carry 20 air-launched cruise missiles (ALCMs), eight internally and 12 externally, to be completed in 1984. The B-52H model will continue to have a penetration role and be armed with nuclear free-fall bombs and AGM-69 short-range attack missiles. It is believed that the B-52 can serve as an efficient and economic stand-off ALCM platform until well into the 1990s. By that time, the USAF plans to have a new

multirole bomber in service to relieve the aged B-52 of all its burdens. Earlier efforts to modernize the bomber force came to naught when the B-70 Valkyrie program was cancelled in 1966 and when President Carter cancelled the B-1 program in 1977 in what many believe was an extremely ill-advised decision.

While standoff aircraft launching salvoes of ALCMs beyond the range of Soviet air defenses are probably the dominant theme in current American thinking about strategic air attack, renewed assault on the air defenses themselves is probable in the future. One proposal is to upgrade SAC's four

Above: the engine of a Boeing AGM-86A air-launched cruise missile ignites after launching from a B-52 carrier aircraft.

Below left: an exploded view of the AGM-86A air-launched cruise missile.

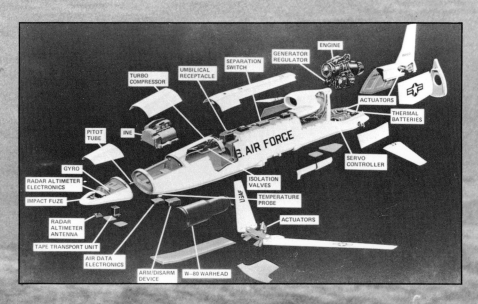

squadrons (65 planes) of FB-111A medium bombers to intercontinental status with new engines, extended range and an enlarged weapons capacity. These would be able to fly some 300mph faster than the 450mph of the lumbering B-52 and have a smaller radar cross section. Whatever new strategic aircraft the United States does field in the 1980s will undoubtedly have the advantage of 'stealth' technologies which came to public notice during the 1980 presidential campaign in a gambit similar to President Johnson's blowing the cover of the SR-71 spy plane during the 1964 campaign. Stealth in fact refers to a number of technologies which have

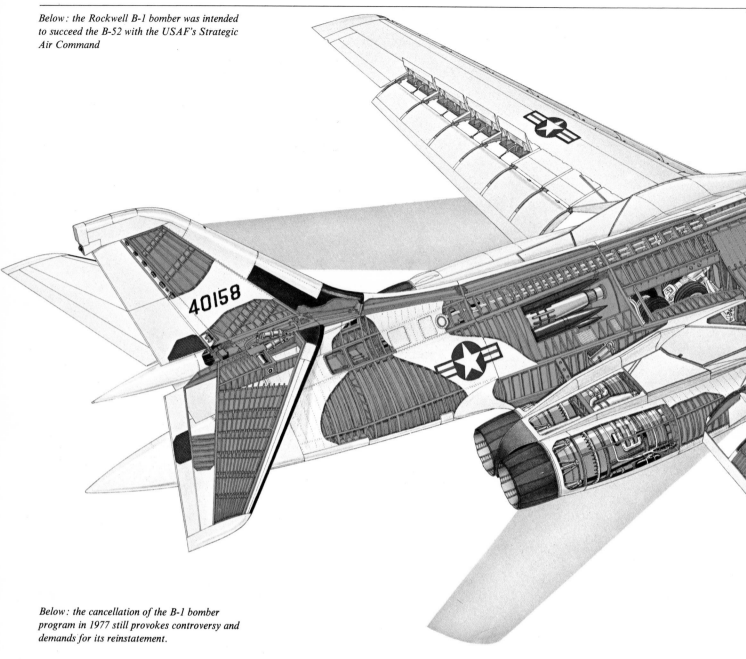

Below: the Rockwell B-1 bomber was intended to succeed the B-52 with the USAF's Strategic Air Command

Below: the cancellation of the B-1 bomber program in 1977 still provokes controversy and demands for its reinstatement.

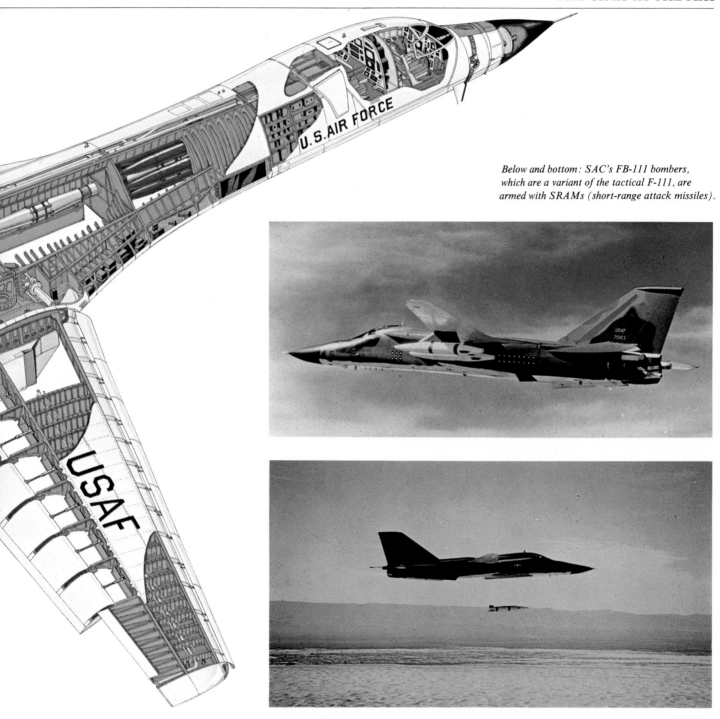

Below and bottom: SAC's FB-111 bombers, which are a variant of the tactical F-111, are armed with SRAMs (short-range attack missiles).

been in development for over 20 years. They involve the use of radar-absorbing materials and designs which scatter radar waves by contouring the aircraft to eliminate flat planes and sharp corners which reflect radar waves. Radar-sensitive parts such as jet air intakes are also repositioned. Other lines of development are designs to prevent the detection of jet engines by infrared sensors. These technologies ultimately could be applied to almost any manned or unmanned aircraft.

Stealth is important because manned bombers, once they penetrate enemy defenses, can cover more targets more flexibly than cruise missiles. If an effective ballistic-missile defense is developed in the next decade or so, manned stand-off and penetrating bombers may resume the primary role in intercontinental nuclear attack at some point in the future at the expense of the ICBM.

Aircraft in World War III will be important but not decisive factors at either the tactical or strategic levels. It has been true from World War II through Vietnam to the most recent Middle East wars that the air superiority of one side makes it markedly more difficult, but not impossible, for the other to operate. The growing ability of air defenses to counter air attack is also making the concept of air superiority more difficult to define. Aircraft thus can have a major impact on battle but they cannot win the war entirely by their own efforts.

World War III will span oceans as well as continents. Naval warfare will play important roles for each side in securing the flanks of the theater in Europe, in controlling the lines of communication between the United States and its allies in Europe and Asia, and in mounting sea-based strategic attacks on the United States and Soviet homelands. Indeed, this latter may well be the most intense aspect of the naval war. Over the past two decades, the missile-launching submarine has emerged as a strategic weapon which is now second only to the ICBM in the threat that it poses to the infrastructure and population of the combatants. Efforts to protect their own missile submarines and attack those of the enemy take a major portion of the naval budgets and forces of the two sides.

Prior to World War II, naval warfare had two primary aspects. One was to attack the enemy's commerce, the other was to engage the enemy battle fleet in major actions to deny it the ability to interfere with movement of troops and operations. The heart of naval warfare was the battleship, a floating gun platform whether it was the wooden ship of the line of Nelson's time or the sleek steel dreadnought of World War I. In both cases, ships engaged each other in long parallel lines with a high volume of gunfire. The battleship was super-seded as the primary engine of naval combat in World War II with the emergence of sea-based combat avia-tion. Prototype aircraft carriers existed in World War I and came to dominate naval warfare early in World War II. The battle of the Coral Sea in 1942 was the first naval engagement in history in which the opposing surface forces never came within sight or gun range of each other. The entire action was conducted by carrier-based strike aircraft. Battle-ships have since been relegated to the shore-bombardment role, as they were used in Korea and Vietnam. At this point, no major power retains a battle-ship in active service. The aircraft decisively replaced the gun as the main naval strike weapon in World War II, but since that time the missile has come to supplant even the aircraft.

The aircraft carrier gave the navy the means to carry the attack to enemy territory, even to the enemy homeland, but since the early 1960s, that role has been taken over by the sea-launched ballistic-missile (SLBM) submarine. The wartime role of the general purpose naval forces for both sides is now to protect the home SLBM forces and attack those of the enemy, to land ground forces where needed and to protect the transfer of supplies and troops. Apart from their changing roles, naval forces themselves have undergone many changes. The size and complexity of ships have sharply increased (except for cruisers, ex-cepted only because that designation is now applied to some large destroyers) but the numbers of ships have sharply decreased. Fewer ships embody far greater offensive and defensive capa-bilities, but characteristics such as speed and maneuverability have decreased in importance because ships serve essentially as platforms to carry weapons and electronic and recon-naissance systems. Ships and sub-marines now have virtually unlimited range due to nuclear propulsion, so the spatial dimension of naval warfare has greatly expanded. Large increases in the range of both weapons and sensors mean that over-the-horizon (OTH) ope-rations are becoming the norm.

Naval warfare now rarely involves one-to-one ship combat but increasingly the integration of surveillance, com-munications, and targeting by surface and submarine platforms and sea- and shore-based aircraft. The newest ships are sailed and fought 'buttoned up' with no one on deck. With the ship sealed against nuclear and chemical attack, all operations are run from a central control room several decks below.

Perhaps the most striking change in naval warfare has been the development of formidable sea-based strategic nuclear capabilities, which have added a new dimension to both nuclear warfare and nuclear deterrence. This in turn has greatly increased the import-ance of other elements of the submarine force and of antisubmarine warfare (ASW) capabilities. This change was brought about by the marriage of the nuclear submarine and the long-range ballistic missile. Nuclear power has eliminated one of the submarine's key weaknesses – the need to surface for air and to charge its batteries. Nuclear submarines need never surface and their increased endurance and speed makes them harder to find and attack.

SLBM submarines are simply sub-merged platforms for ballistic missiles but it is only in recent years that SLBMs have gained true ICBM ranges of between 4000–5000 miles. Early SLBMs had ranges of only a few hundred miles. The Soviet SS-N-5 and SS-N-6 SLBMs have a range of 700 and 1500 miles respectively and the United States Polaris and Poseidon missiles 1500 and 2500 miles. In the early 1970s,

Overleaf: a Talos SAM is fired from a warship.

Below: a US missile submarine's control room.

the Soviet Union introduced the SS-N-8 with a range of over 4200 miles and subsequently the SS-N-18 with a range of around 5400 miles. In late 1979 the first US Navy boat, the *Francis Scott Key*, to carry 4000-mile Trident I SLBMs went on patrol. Increased range is important because it greatly reduces the vulnerability of the submarine. The earlier boats with short-range missiles had to patrol in limited forward areas to be within range of their targets and were therefore easier to detect. Longer range missiles make possible immense broad ocean patrol areas, as favored by the United States, or deployment in home waters under the protection of other naval forces, as favored by the Soviet Union.

SLBMs differ from ICBMs in other important operational ways. As they are launched from tubes in submarines, SLBM size is constrained. Warhead yields are thus smaller, as is the amount of other equipment with which SLBMs can be provided. SLBMs are 'cold-launched' – the boat is rolled slightly to one side and the missile ejected by compressed gas before the engine ignites. Rolling the boat is a precaution to ensure that the missile does not fall back on the boat in the event of failure. The early submarines had to surface to launch but modern boats all launch submerged. SLBMs are not as accurate as ICBMs because they are launched from moving platforms. SLBMs have thus always been considered soft-target weapons, but accuracy has been steadily improving. There are still no hard-target SLBMs but the United States Trident II missile, if it is built, would be the first as the technology is now available. SLBMs can by MIRVed, as are the Soviet SS-N-18 and the American Poseidon and Trident I missiles. SLBMs with ICBM ranges have the same time to target (approximately 30 minutes) after launch, but shorter range forward-deployed missiles can be on target in less than five

Right: A missile loading technician prepares to take on nuclear missiles for the USS Calhoun *submarine at Charleston Navy Yard.*

Above right: a Polaris A-3 SLBM is launched from the USS Patrick Henry. *The Polaris was the first US SLBM and is also used by the UK.*

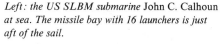
Left: the US SLBM submarine John C. Calhoun at sea. The missile bay with 16 launchers is just aft of the sail.

Below left: the Soviet Victor class fleet submarine is nuclear-powered and is fitted with eight torpedo tubes.

Bottom left: Soviet Delta I class nuclear-powered submarines carry the 4800 nautical mile range SS-N-8 SLBM.

minutes, which provides no usable warning time at all.

The Soviet Union has a long history of interest in SLBMs, dating back to 1945 when the Russians became aware of German research in this area. The first Soviet SLBM launch was in 1955 from a modified Zulu class diesel submarine and was followed by the Golf class SLBM and the Hotel class nuclear SLBM submarine. In 1967, the Soviets deployed 34 Yankee class nuclear boats carrying 16 1300 to 1600-mile SS-N-6s and began regular patrols off the east and west coasts of the United States. In 1972, the Delta class made its appearance with the Delta I, essentially the Yankee design modified to carry 12 SS-N-8 missiles. The Delta II boats carry 16 SS-N-8s while the Delta IIIs, the newest model, carry 16 SS-N-18 missiles.

The first United States SLBM submarine patrol put to sea in the Atlantic in 1960. A Mediterranean patrol began in 1963 and Far Eastern patrols from Guam started in 1964. The United

Right: Soviet Charlie class submarines are cruise-missile attack boats carrying eight SS-N-7 missiles. They first appeared in 1967.

Below right: a Soviet Echo II class cruise-missile submarine on patrol. This nuclear-powered boat carries eight cruise missiles.

States has built five classes of SLBM submarines: the *George Washington* (SSBN 598) with 16 Polaris missiles, operational in 1959; the *Ethan Allen* (SSBN 608) with 16 Polaris missiles, operational in 1961 and the *Lafayette* (SSBN 616), *James Madison* (SSBN 627) and *Benjamin Franklin* (SSBN 640), all with 16 Poseidon missiles and operational in 1963, 1964 and 1965. Of the 31 Poseidon boats, three have already been converted to carry Trident I missiles and nine more are scheduled for conversion. The Polaris boats are scheduled for conversion to attack submarines from the early 1980s as the *Ohio* Class (SSBN 726) of eight boats carrying 24 Trident I missiles with 12 MIRVs apiece begins to come into service. The *Ohio* Class boats are exceptionally large and powerful and mark a quantum jump over earlier SSBN designs. The Soviet Union is bringing out the Typhoon Class, believed to be roughly equivalent to the *Ohio* in size and firepower, in the early 1980s.

Britain and France also have SLBM forces. The former deploys four *Resolution* Class boats each carrying 16 Polaris missiles. The missiles were modernized in 1980 with a new British-designed warhead called Chevaline with a one-megaton yield. Five new boats will replace the *Resolution* Class in the 1990s and carry the Trident I missile. France has 80 SLBMs in five *Redoutable* Class boats. These are also scheduled for modernization in the 1980s on a one-for-one basis, with the new M-4 SLBM to replace the current M-20.

Strategic nuclear arms have thus increasingly been put to sea as each side has built up and then modernized powerful SLBM forces. This fact was recognized in SALT I which placed a limit of 62 modern (Yankee and Delta) boats and 950 modern launch tubes on the USSR and 44 boats and 710 launch tubes on the United States. The United States has in fact never deployed more than 41 boats and 656 tubes and the number of boats will shrink slowly during the 1980s under current pro-

Below: a Soviet Foxtrot class torpedo attack submarine underway in the Mediterranean. This is an older class of diesel-powered boat.

grams. SALT II would remove the differences in force size by placing on each side an overall ceiling on strategic launchers, with each side free to choose the proportion of ICBMs, SLBMs and bombers in its strategic forces.

Despite the inaccuracy of SLBMs, their attraction is that they are believed to be invulnerable to attack because their launch platforms are mobile and submerged. They are thus believed to give each side an assured second strike or retaliatory strike capability and play a central role in strategic nuclear deterrence. As ICBMs are increasingly thought to be less survivable and thus less deterring, the attractiveness of SLBMs has been growing, especially as the prospect of hard-target SLBMs grows nearer.

The invulnerability of SLBMs, however, is really dependent on the ASW capabilities of general purpose naval forces and the concomitant ability of these forces to protect their own SLBM submarines from attack. Dealing with the enemy's SLBM submarines and protecting its own are probably the two highest priority naval missions of each side. The problem is to locate the boats precisely enough to destroy them. The location can be attempted by surface ships, submarines, aircraft and various permanent and temporary sensors.

The principal means of submarine detection is still sonar in one form or another. Sonar is the measurement of the direction and return time of sound echoes. Passive sonars listen to the sounds coming in, whereas active sonars send out sound emissions and measure the reflections. Active sonar is more accurate but can betray the position and presence of its platform. Passive sonar is more difficult to use and sometimes can be interfered with by the noise of its own or neighboring ships. Major advances in signal processing now make possible the extraction of weaker and more ambiguous signals from incoming noise. Detection range and the ability to identify the noise emitter as a submarine have therefore substantially increased. Large arrays of hydrophones are also towed on the surface and aircraft and helicopters can seed given areas with hydrophones in sonobuoys to localize the position of a target in a smaller area. However, sound waves are not always good indicators of location and range because variations in water temperatures can distort their direction. In shallow zones sound does not travel at times, and sometimes freak long-range detection can occur and then cease. The physics of sound transmission in the oceans is complex and not well understood yet. The

United States has a clear and long-standing advantage over the USSR in this area because of superior signal-processing capabilities and much quieter nuclear boats.

Detection is the first part of the problem and attack is the second. There is a wide variety of weapons which are effective against submarines. Nuclear-powered attack submarines armed with torpedoes are considered by far the most effective ASW instrument by both sides. Attack submarines can be used in barrier operations to prevent enemy naval forces from penetrating certain areas or as screens for convoys and task forces. They can be equipped with both torpedoes and antisubmarine and anti-ship missiles. The Soviets have long equipped about half of their nuclear-powered submarine force with missiles. Modern attack boats place a high value on maneuverability to attack and escape. All torpedo tubes are now placed in the bow to give a better hydrodynamic profile. The maneuvering ability of both boats and the torpedoes themselves makes stern tubes unnecessary.

The United States has some 70 nuclear-powered attack submarines, including 12 *Los Angeles* Class (SSN 668). These are 9000-ton boats armed with submarine-launched antisubmarine rocket (SUBROC) ASW torpedoes and the Harpoon antiship missile. These began to enter service in 1976 with a total force of 35 envisioned. Also 37 *Sturgeon* and 13 *Thresher* Class boats are armed with SUBROC. The Soviets

Left: the Soviet aircraft carrier Minsk *cruises off the coast of the Republic of the Philippines in 1979, with Yakovlev Forgers on the flight deck.*

Above: the Soviet aircraft carrier Kiev, *sister ship of the* Minsk, *underway in the Mediterranean. Kamov Ka-25 Hormone ASW helicopters are carried.*

have invested heavily in cruise-missile as well as torpedo-attack boats and have some 46 nuclear-powered boats of the former and 45 of the latter. The Soviet Union also has 23 diesel-powered cruise-missile boats, all old and probably not far from retirement, and 143 diesel torpedo-attack submarines. Many of these are old and some were designed only for service in coastal waters. The Soviet Union has an active building program and both the nuclear and diesel forces are being modernized. Yankee class boats required under SALT I to be deactivated as SLBM platforms are also believed to have been converted to attack boats to augment the purpose-built forces.

Other nuclear-powered attack submarines which would be a factor in operations in the North Atlantic and adjacent waters are the 11 British boats of the *Swiftsure, Valiant* and *Dreadnought* Classes. Since 1976 the French have had a program for nuclear attack boats, with the first to be launched in 1981. The other NATO members deploy only diesel boats, some of very good design and capability, for use in local waters. Some of the non-Soviet Warsaw Pact members deploy a few old Soviet diesel boats.

Surface forces and shore- and sea-based aircraft have played important roles in ASW operations since World

Right and above right: the Soviet aircraft carrier Minsk *is pictured operating her Yakovlev Forger V/STOL aircraft.*

Above: the Tu-22M Backfire bomber is becoming one of the most important strike weapons of the Soviet Navy. Note the nose-mounted in-flight refuelling probe.

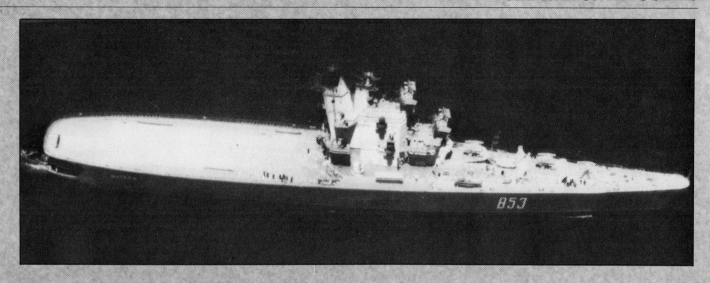

Above: the 18,000-ton Moskva *Class helicopter cruisers, carrying 18 Ka-25 Hormone helicopters, were the forerunners of the Kiev Class aircraft carriers. Two were built between 1967–69.*

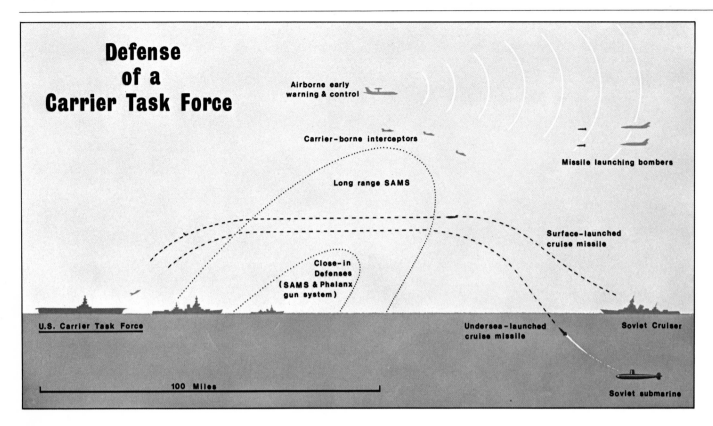

Defense of a Carrier Task Force

Airborne early warning & control

Carrier-borne interceptors

Missile launching bombers

Long range SAMS

Surface-launched cruise missile

Close-in Defenses (SAMS & Phalanx gun system)

U.S. Carrier Task Force

Undersea-launched cruise missile

Soviet Cruiser

100 Miles

Soviet submarine

Above: a diagram which illustrates the layered defense of a US carrier task force against Soviet air and standoff missile attack.

War II. Indeed, the Soviet navy is basically oriented toward ASW missions to defend the homeland against sea-based nuclear attack and to protect the Soviet sea-based nuclear deterrent. The early Soviet naval strategy was to defend against seaborne invasion. This led to the development of a large coastal force covered by strong shore-based airpower. Subsequently, nuclear strikes by western carrier-based forces became the greatest threat and led to a reliance on long-range shore-based aviation and heavy investment in attack submarines and larger surface ships armed with cruise missiles. The USSR pioneered the development and use of naval cruise missiles, probably because these weapons offered a quick and cheap solution to the problem of acquiring effective antiship firepower. It was probably fairly easy for the Soviet Union to make this innovation because they did not have large current investments in gun-armed ships. The Soviet navy has already deployed six classes of naval cruise missiles, on everything from fast patrol boats to submarines and

their newer guided-missile destroyers and cruisers. The advent of the SLBM made it the primary threat and has since led to a concentration on ASW platforms and capabilities.

One important trend in Soviet naval policy has been to extend the range of its defense, first in response to the longer ranges of carrier aircraft and then the much longer ranges of SLBMs. The result has been a trend toward larger, more seaworthy ships and in recent years sea-based aviation. In the late 1950s, the Soviets built two *Moskva* Class cruisers which carried ASW helicopters and in the early 1970s began construction of a class of small ASW carriers which are equipped with ASW helicopters and Yak-36 Forger V/STOL aircraft. Known as the *Kiev* Class after the first unit, two units are in commission, a third is being built and a fourth is planned, which is believed to be the final one of the program. It is widely believed by western analysts that sometime within the next decade the Soviet Union will launch a large-deck carrier. The Soviet Union is also building a class of superlarge (25,000 tons, estimated) cruiser, termed the *Kirov* Class, which is heavily armed for ASW, antiship and air-defense missions.

Right: the British Invincible Class aircraft carriers will operate V/STOL Sea Harriers for air defense, reconnaissance and strike duties.

The Soviets also astonished western analysts in 1980 by launching the world's largest submarine, the Oscar class cruise-missile boat, which is formidably armed for antiship missions.

These forces provide ASW protection against Western SLBM submarines and protect Soviet SSBNs from Western ASW forces. The broad outline of Soviet wartime operations apparently is to hold its Delta (and eventually Typhoon) class boats with their long-range missiles in home waters such as the Barents Sea and further out

Below: the Yankee class were the first Soviet SLBM submarines and carried 16 SS-N-6 SLBMs in launch tubes behind the sail.

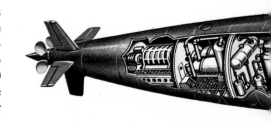

Above: a US carrier battle group steams in the Arabian Sea with attendant escorts and supply ships. It was dispatched during the Iranian crisis.

in the Norwegian Sea where other Soviet naval forces and shore-based aviation can support them against NATO ASW. The SS-N-8 and SS-N-18 can cover targets in the United States quite well from these areas. This means that other Soviet naval forces must have capabilities against NATO attack submarines, carrier task groups and airborne ASW forces. The Soviet Union has placed main reliance on nuclear attack submarines but believes the best results stem from operation of these units as part of a coordinated force with surface units and aviation. The range and striking power of shore-based aviation has notably increased since the mid-1970s when the Tu-22M Backfire bomber began to enter Soviet Naval Aviation. NATO carrier groups must now come within range of the formidable Backfire to attack Soviet SSBNs or to launch nuclear-strike aircraft against Soviet territory. One major area of naval operations will in all likelihood be along the Greenland-Iceland-UK gap which is a logical avenue of attack for NATO forces and an equally logical place for Soviet forward defenses.

Conditioned by the two world wars, Westerners tend to see the large Soviet attack submarine force as a primary threat to the lines of communication between North America and Europe. Most of these boats would be effective against shipping, but they would be operating unsupported over 2500 miles from their nearest base against strong ASW forces. Soviet military writers have identified the failure of the German antishipping campaigns as being due to the lack of support for the submarines. It is unlikely that the Soviets, in face of the very substantial Western naval threat to their homeland, would divert boats from the primary anti-SSBN and anticarrier missions. In any event it would be more effective to attack ports and depots rather than the shipping itself.

In the 1950s the United States and its NATO allies had an immense advantage over the USSR in general-purpose naval forces and still maintain a considerable advantage in quality of weaponry and ship characteristics. Although the USSR now has a slightly larger number of ships than the United States, it is out-

Top right: two Terrier SAMs mounted on the guided-missile cruiser USS Leahy.

Above right: a Soviet Kresta II *cruiser shadows NATO ships during a major exercise.*

Right: the Soviet nuclear-powered guided-missile cruiser Kirov *carries out sea trials in 1980. The ship is large and heavily armed.*

Below: NATO's Standing Naval Force Atlantic, *which includes ships from several allied navies, is pictured at sea in 1980.*

has declined considerably, their ships are high-technology products with multimission capabilities. A good example is the US Navy's new Aegis Class (CG-47) guided-missile cruiser. These 8800-ton $780,000,000 ships have a computer-controlled, radar-directed defense system which can transmit in all directions simultaneously and detect, track and engage incoming missiles while still searching for others. The fire-control system automatically launches the new Standard SM-2 missile and guides it by radar to a point near the target. The missile's own radar seeker then takes over. Should this system fail to stop all missiles, the Phalanx close-in

Below: the aircraft carrier USS Independence at sea in the Atlantic. Her wing comprises some 90 fighter, attack, ASW and other aircraft.

numbered by the combined navies of the three main naval powers of NATO, Britain, France and the United States. Parsimony in defense matters has greatly reduced the size and power of the Royal Navy from the 17 attack carriers of the mid-1950s to several small ASW carriers in 1980. The United States fleet has been halved, from 955 ships in 1960 to some 450 in active service in 1980. The United States began a five-year shipbuilding program in 1980 aimed at adding 95 new ships with the emphasis on guided-missile ships for air defense. The British and French navies, with 70 and 48 major surface combat vessels respectively, are also undergoing some modernization.

Though the size of the NATO navies

Below: HMS Battleaxe *is one of the Royal Navy's* Broadsword *Class frigates and carries a single Westland Lynx ASW and antiship helicopter.*

Right: the Soviet Krivak Class guided-missile destroyers are among the most heavily armed warships of their size in the world.

air-defense system, an all-weather automatically controlled gun system will throw up a high-density screen of radar-directed pellets to knock the missile down. The Aegis Class will also mount two Harpoon antiship missile launchers and carry ASW helicopters which can provide early warning of targets beyond the ship's radar horizons and guide missiles to those targets. The mission of these complex ships is to protect aircraft carriers from submarine, aircraft and missile attacks. The navy has a minimum

Below: the British destroyer HMS Bristol *launches a Sea Dart missile. Sea Dart is an area-defense system against high/low air attack.*

requirement of 1.5 Aegis cruisers for each of the 12 aircraft carriers in service and their battle groups.

The heart of United States naval power is still the large-deck attack carrier, of which there are now 13. Normally, four are deployed, eight are in transit, training or overhaul and one is in the two-year-long service-life-extension program intended to add another 15 years of service life. There are 10 conventional carriers of the *Kitty Hawk, Kennedy, Forrestal* and *Midway* Classes and three 90,000-ton nuclear-powered *Enterprise* and *Nimitz* Class ships. Two more *Nimitz* Class ships are under construction and will

join the fleet in 1983 and 1987. The United States operates its carriers in task groups. A typical task group in the 1980s might include two *Oliver Hazard Perry* Class (FFG-7) guided-missile frigates, two Aegis Class cruisers, two other guided-weapons cruisers such as the nuclear-powered *Virginia* Class, and two gun/guided weapons destroyers of perhaps the *Spruance* Class. The carrier task group is a formidable concentration of offensive and defensive power which includes some 90 attack, ASW, reconnaissance, ECM, early-warning and even tanker planes.

The two primary missions of these task groups are to conduct strikes

Above: the US Navy's EA-6B Prowler is an ECM aircraft. Electronic countermeasures and ECCM will be important factors in the war at sea.

against the USSR and to conduct ASW. Prior to the mid-1970s, some groups were assigned primarily nuclear-strike missions and others primarily ASW missions. Partly in the interests of economy and partly for flexibility, all carriers now have dual ASW and nuclear-attack missions. To support the ASW mission, the navy has developed the Antisubmarine Warfare Center Command and Control System, a worldwide network providing target data drawn from fixed undersea networks of passive hydrophone detector arrays around the United States and from mobile detection systems as well.

The primary threat to the carrier stems not from close-in attack by manned aircraft but from the large numbers of missiles which will be launched from Soviet aerial, surface and submerged platforms. The new Soviet Oscar class cruise-missile submarine in particular is thought to be capable of heavy firepower as it is fitted with the SS-NX-19, a new antiship missile. The air defense of the carrier groups will extend for hundreds of miles, with airborne warning and control systems (AWACS) on patrol supported by a few long-range interceptors. When the AWACS detect Soviet aircraft, more interceptors will be launched to attempt to shoot down the Soviet bombers, likely to be Backfire or Badgers but they could be naval

Bears, before they can launch their missiles. The Phoenix AIM-54 missile of the F-14 has a range of 130 miles for this mission. Any Soviet missiles which are launched will first face a long-range area defense of SAMs like the Standard SM-1, replacing the earlier Talos and Terrier, at 55km and the new Standard SM-2 of the Aegis system. British and French long-range SAMs are the Sea Dart and the older Sea Slug and Masurca, all with a range of 45km. Close-in defense is provided by guns and short-range, quick-reaction SAMs like the British Seacat, French Crotale and American Tartar and Sea Sparrow. The task group can also counterattack the Soviet forces with its own aircraft, missiles and submarines.

All missiles fired at the task group will be PGMs, but firepower will still be important and indeed the missiles may have to be salvoed for some to penetrate a modern, layered air defense such as Aegis. As the standoff ranges at which missiles are launched continue to lengthen, the time available for detection and countermeasures also lengthens. Seymour Deitchman has calculated that 50 missiles would have to be fired for 3.5 to reach the target for an average of 0.4 hits per ship. A large ship like a carrier will require a number of hits to be put out of action. There is also the question of how accurately radars and missile seekers can distinguish the carrier as the main target in a group of ships. Missiles may in fact acquire and attack the wrong target. Antiship and ASW missiles

Left: an Exocet surface-to-surface antiship missile is fired from a French warship. It has a range of some 40km.

Below left: the air-to-surface version of Exocet is fired from a Super Frelon helicopter of the French Navy.

Below: a fast patrol boat of the Greek Navy launches an Exocet. Such craft are useful for the defense of coastal waters.

Right: a US Navy F-14 Tomcat fleet-defense fighter in flight with its VG wing fully swept back. The F-14's radar can detect targets at a range of 100 nautical miles.

Above: a Tomahawk cruise missile is fired from an armored box launcher installed in the destroyer USS Merrill. *This launcher can carry up to four cruise missiles.*

Right: a Tomahawk sea-launched cruise missile emerges from the water under boost motor power, following launch from a torpedo tube of the nuclear-powered submarine USS Guitarro.

Above: a Harpoon missile is fired from the escort ship USS Knox. The Harpoon is the first US antiship cruise missile.

can and do use nuclear warheads but even an attack with nuclear missiles, not lightly expendable commodities, would have to be substantial as Deitchman points out.

There are thus many unknowns in high-technology war at sea but guided missiles will be effective weapons nonetheless. There are few important targets and these have strong radar and infrared signatures without the background clutter found on land. OTH attack by

unmanned weapons requires continuing data on target location since the targets almost by definition are moving. Long-range aircraft and satellites are thus important elements in the sea battle. Nuclear warheads can be used at sea to good effect because their large radii of effects reduces the degree of accuracy necessary for conventional weapons. Water attenuates the radiation effects and no fallout is produced, hence some analysts have speculated that each side would tolerate the use of nuclear torpedoes, missiles and depth charges in the sea war in a way which would cause an escalation to general

nuclear war if they were so freely used in the war on the land.

The war of the oceans will be a high-technology, electronically intense conflict revolving around submarines, aircraft and missiles. The United States and NATO will face a sustained long-range air and submarine attack which western ASW and air-defense capabilities will undoubtedly make expensive for the Soviet Union but which could be effective. In the foreseeable future the Soviet Union has little chance of success in hunting Trident-armed SSBNs, which have all of the Atlantic and much of the Pacific and Indian Oceans as cover. NATO success in dealing with the long-range missile-armed Soviet Delta and Typhoon class boats will be directly related to success in dealing with Soviet general and long-range aircraft assigned to their protection. NATO should win the war of the oceans because the United States, Britain and France are historically maritime powers possessing modern, well-balanced naval forces. The military potency of the Soviet navy, on the other hand, suffers from its strong ASW orientation, its almost complete lack of sea-based air power, weak high-seas logistics capabilities and its general lack of broad experience in the operational aspects of naval warfare. Experience is not gained overnight nor does naval force structure change rapidly, so this situation will continue for quite some time.

GLOSSARY

AA Anti Aircraft
ABM Anti Ballistic Missile
AGM Air to Ground Missile
ALCM Air Launched Cruise Missile
APDSFS Armor Piercing Discarding Sabot Fin Stabilized
ARM Anti Radiation Missile
ASM Air to Surface Missile
ASW Anti Submarine Warfare
ATGM Anti Tank Guided Missile
AWACS Airborne Warning and Control System
AZON (bomb guided in) AZimuth ONly
C³ Command, Control and Communications
CEP Circular Error Probable
CIA Central Intelligence Agency
COMSAT COMmunication SATellite
DEW Distant Early Warning
DIVAD DIVision Air Defense
DSCS Defense Satellite Communications System
ECM Electronic Counter Measures
ECCM Electronic Counter Counter Measures
EHF Extra High Frequency
EMP Electro Magnetic Pulse
ENIAC Electronic Numerical Integrator and Calculator
FEBA Forward Edge of the Battle Area
FOBS Fractional Orbital Bombardment System
FROG Free Rocket Over Ground

GLCM Ground Launched Cruise Missile
HEAT High Explosive Anti Tank
HEP High Explosive Plastic (British, HESH High Explosive Squash Head)
HOBO Homing Optical BOmb
ICBM Inter Continental Ballistic Missile
ICM Improved Conventional Munition
IRBM Intermediate Range Ballistic Missile
IUS Inertial Upper Stage
KE Kinetic Energy
LASER Light Amplification by Stimulated Emission of Radiation
LOTW Launch on Tactical Warning
LRTNF Long Range Theater Nuclear Forces
MAD Mutual Assured Destruction
MAPS Multiple Aim Points System
MHV Miniature Homing Vehicle
MICV Mechanized Infantry Combat Vehicle
MIRV Multiple Independently Targeted Reentry Vehicle
MLRS Multiple Launch Rocket System
MX Missile Experimental
NASA National Aeronautics and Space Authority
NATO North Atlantic Treaty Organization
NBC Nuclear Bacteriological Chemical
NORAD NOrth American Air Defense Command
NSA National Security Agency
OTH Over The Horizon

PAR Perimeter Acquisition Radar
PBV Post Boost Vehicle
PGM Precision Guided Munition
RPV Remotely Piloted Vehicle
RV Reentry Vehicle
SAC Strategic Air Command
SALT Strategic Arms Limitation Talks
SAM Surface to Air Missile
SHF Super High Frequency
SIGINT SIGnals INTelligence
SIOP Single Integrated Operations Plan
SLAR Side Looking Airborne Radar
SLBM Sea Launched Ballistic Missile
SRAM Short Range Attack Missile
SRF Strategic Rocket Forces
SS Surface to Surface
STAFF Smart Target Activated Fire and Forget
SUBROC SUBmarine launched antisubmarine ROCket
TERCOM TERrain COntour Matching
TOW Tubed launched Optically tracked Wire guided
UHF Ultra High Frequency
VGW Variable Geometry Wing (or 'swing wing')
VHF Very High Frequency
V/STOL Vertical/Short Take Off and Landing
WWMCCS World Wide Military Command and Control System

ACKNOWLEDGMENTS

Picture Acknowledgments
Aérospatiale: pp 10–11, 12 (upper right).
Author's collection: pp 8 (upper), 9, 14 (upper), 15, 68, 72–73, 98, 114 (upper), 116, 122, 128 (lower), 130–131 (upper), 132–133, 134 (lower), 136, 137, 138–139, 155 (lower), 156 (lower), 175.
Boeing: p 31 (upper).
British Aerospace Dynamics: pp 12–13, 184–185.
David Brown Gears, via *Defence*: p 179 (center).
Defence pp 12 (upper left), 186 (upper and center).
FMC Corp: p 126 (center).
General Dynamics: pp 6–7, 23 (lower), 188, 188–189.
Hughes Helicopters: pp 148–149.
Martin Marietta Aerospace: pp 10 (upper), 101 (upper right).
Ministry of Defence: pp 13 (upper), 16–17, 180

(center), 180–181, 183.
NASA: p 76 (lower).
Plessey Marine: pp 182–183.
Rockwell International: pp 84 (upper), 149.
Solartron: p 20 (upper).
Thomson-CFS: pp 186–187.
USAF: pp 26–27, 28, 29, 30, 31 (lower), 32–33, 34–35, 36, 37, 38, 39 (lower), 40–41, 42–43, 44–45, 46–47, 51 (upper two), 52–53, 54–55, 58–59, 60–61, 63 (upper), 64–65, 66–67, 69, 70, 71, 74, 75, 76 (upper), 77, 78, 79, 80, 81, 82–83, 84–85, 88–89, 90–91, 94, 95, 96–97, 99, 100, 101 (upper left), 102–103, 109, 138 (center), 142–143, 144, 145, 146–147, 150, 151 (lower), 152, 154 (upper), 155 (upper and center), 160 (upper), 161, 162–163, 164–165, 166, 167, 170, 171, 177.
US Army: pp 11 (upper), 14 (lower), 20–21, 22, 48–49,

51 (lower), 56–57, 62–63, 86–87, 104, 105, 106, 107, 108, 110–111, 112, 113, 114–115, 117, 118–119, 120–121, 123 (upper), 124–125, 126–127, 128 (upper and center), 129, 130–131, 132, 133, 135, 138 (upper), 139, 141, 147 (lower), 148, 156 (upper and center), 157, 158–159, 160 (lower).
US Navy: pp 8 (lower), 16 (upper), 17 (upper), 18–19, 24–25, 151 (center), 152–153, 168–169, 172–173, 174, 174–175, 176–177, 179 (upper), 180 (upper and lower).
Vought Corp: pp 23 (upper), 134 (upper), 140.

Artworks
Peter Endsleigh Castle: pp 39, 101 (lower), 123, 151 (upper), 154, 178, 178–179.
P. Cannings: pp 92–93.
M. Badrocke: pp 150–151, 166–167.